# Professional Examinations

# AQ2016

## Using Accounting Software

# EXAM KIT

This Exam Kit supports study for the following AAT qualifications:

AAT Foundation Certificate in Accounting – Level 2
AAT Foundation Diploma in Accounting and Business – Level 2
AAT Foundation Certificate in Bookkeeping – Level 2
AAT Foundation Award in Accounting Software – Level 2
AAT Level 2 Award in Accounting Skills to Run Your Business
AAT Foundation Certificate in Accounting at SCQF Level 5

KAPLAN

PUBLISHING

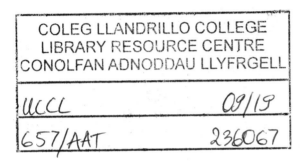
**British Library Cataloguing-in-Publication Data**

A catalogue record for this book is available from the British Library.

Published by:

Kaplan Publishing UK

Unit 2 The Business Centre

Molly Millar's Lane

Wokingham

Berkshire

RG41 2QZ

ISBN: 978-1-78740-282-9

© Kaplan Financial Limited, 2018

Printed and bound in Great Britain.

Kaplan P...... .........tly finding new
ways to r................ ur studies and our
exciting ...................... do offer something
differe......................... exam success.

236067

LANDRI... 9

This book comes with free MyKaplan online resources so that you can study anytime, anywhere. **This free online resource is not sold separately and is included in the price**

Having purchased this book, you have access to the following online study ma

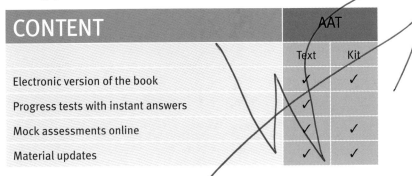

| CONTENT | AAT | |
| --- | --- | --- |
| | Text | Kit |
| Electronic version of the book | ✓ | ✓ |
| Progress tests with instant answers | ✓ | |
| Mock assessments online | ✓ | ✓ |
| Material updates | ✓ | ✓ |

**hunan wasanaeth
self service**

236067

### How to access your online resources

Kaplan Financial students will already have a MyKaplan account and these extra resources wi
you online. You do not need to register again, as this process was completed when you enrol
problems accessing online materials, please ask your course administrator.

If you are not studying with Kaplan and did not purchase your book via a Kaplan website, to u
resources please go to www.mykaplan.co.uk/addabook (even if you have set up an account a
previously). You will then need to enter the ISBN number (on the title page and back cover) and ....... .......... ........,
number contained in the scratch panel below to gain access. You will also be required to enter additional information
during this process to set up or confirm your account details.

If you purchased through Kaplan Flexible Learning or via the Kaplan Publishing website you will automatically receive
an e-mail invitation to MyKaplan. Please register your details using this email to gain access to your content. If you do
not receive the e-mail or book content, please contact Kaplan Publishing.

### Your Code and Information

This code can only be used once for the registration of one book online. This registration and your online content will
expire when the final sittings for the examinations covered by this book have taken place. Please allow one hour from
the time you submit your book details for us to process your request.

Please scratch the film to access your MyKaplan code.

Please be aware that this code is case-sensitive and you will need to include the dashes
within the passcode, but not when entering the ISBN. For further technical support,
please visit www.MyKaplan.co.uk

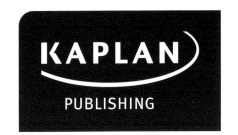

# CONTENTS

**Features in this exam kit**

In addition to providing a wide ranging bank of real exam style questions, we have also included in this kit:

- Paper specific information and advice on exam technique.

- Our recommended approach to make your revision for this particular subject as effective as possible.

You will find a wealth of other resources to help you with your studies on MyKaplan and AAT websites:

www.mykaplan.co.uk

www.aat.org.uk/

Quality and accuracy are of the utmost importance to us so if you spot an error in any of our products, please send an email to mykaplanreporting@kaplan.com with full details, or follow the link to the feedback form in MyKaplan.

Our Quality Co-ordinator will work with our technical team to verify the error and take action to ensure it is corrected in future editions.

# UNIT-SPECIFIC INFORMATION

## THE EXAM

### FORMAT OF THE ASSESSMENT

The assessment will consist of one part and will cover the learning outcomes listed in the table below.

In any one assessment, students may not be assessed on all content, or on the full depth or breadth of a  piece of content. The content assessed may change over time to ensure validity of assessment, but all assessment criteria will be tested over time.

The learning outcomes for this unit are as follows:

| | Learning outcome | Weighting |
|---|---|---|
| 1 | Set up accounting software | 25% |
| 2 | Process sales and purchases transactions | 35% |
| 3 | Process bank and cash transactions | 20% |
| 4 | Perform period end routine tasks | 15% |
| 5 | Produce reports | 5% |
| | Total | 100% |

**Time allowed**

2 hours

### PASS MARK

The pass mark for all AAT CBAs is 70%.

 **Always keep your eye on the clock and make sure you attempt all questions!**

## DETAILED SYLLABUS

The detailed syllabus and study guide written by the AAT can be found at:

www.aat.org.uk/

# INDEX TO PRACTICE QUESTIONS

# EXAM TECHNIQUE

- **Do not skip any of the material** in the syllabus.

- **Read each question** *very* carefully.

- **Double-check your answer** before committing yourself to it.

- Answer **every** question – if you do not know an answer to a multiple choice question or true/false question, you don't lose anything by guessing. Think carefully before you **guess**.

- If you are answering a multiple-choice question, **eliminate first those answers that you know are wrong**. Then choose the most appropriate answer from those that are left.

- **Don't panic** if you realise you've answered a question incorrectly. Getting one question wrong will not mean the difference between passing and failing

## Computer-based exams – tips

- Do not attempt a CBA until you have **completed all study material** relating to it.

- On the AAT website there is a CBA demonstration. It is **ESSENTIAL** that you attempt this before your real CBA. You will become familiar with how to move around the CBA screens and the way that questions are formatted, increasing your confidence and speed in the actual exam.

- Be sure you understand how to use the **software** before you start the exam. If in doubt, ask the assessment centre staff to explain it to you.

- Questions are **displayed on the screen** and answers are entered using keyboard and mouse. At the end of the exam, you are given a certificate showing the result you have achieved.

- In addition to the traditional multiple-choice question type, CBAs will also contain **other types of questions**, such as number entry questions, drag and drop, true/false, pick lists or drop down menus or hybrids of these.

- In some CBAs you will have to type in complete computations or written answers.

- You need to be sure you **know how to answer questions** of this type before you sit the exam, through practice.

KAPLAN PUBLISHING

# KAPLAN'S RECOMMENDED REVISION APPROACH

## QUESTION PRACTICE IS THE KEY TO SUCCESS

Success in professional examinations relies upon you acquiring a firm grasp of the required knowledge at the tuition phase. In order to be able to do the questions, knowledge is essential.

However, the difference between success and failure often hinges on your exam technique on the day and making the most of the revision phase of your studies.

The **Kaplan Study Text** is the starting point, designed to provide the underpinning knowledge to tackle all questions. However, in the revision phase, poring over text books is not the answer.

**Kaplan Pocket Notes** are designed to help you quickly revise a topic area; however you then need to practise questions. There is a need to progress to exam style questions as soon as possible, and to tie your exam technique and technical knowledge together.

**The importance of question practice cannot be over-emphasised.**

The recommended approach below is designed by expert tutors in the field, in conjunction with their knowledge of the examiner and the specimen assessment.

**You need to practise as many questions as possible in the time you have left.**

## OUR AIM

Our aim is to get you to the stage where you can attempt exam questions confidently, to time, in a closed book environment, with no supplementary help (i.e. to simulate the real examination experience).

Practising your exam technique is also vitally important for you to assess your progress and identify areas of weakness that may need more attention in the final run up to the examination.

In order to achieve this we recognise that initially you may feel the need to practice some questions with open book help.

**Good exam technique is vital.**

# THE KAPLAN UACS REVISION PLAN

## Stage 1: Assess areas of strengths and weaknesses

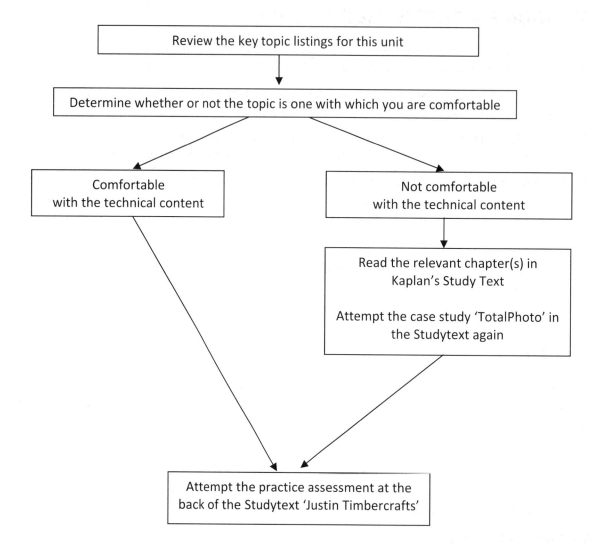

## Stage 2: Practice scenarios

Follow the order of practice scenarios as presented in this Kit and attempt the questions in the order suggested.

Try to avoid referring to Study Texts and your notes and the model answer until you have completed your attempt.

Review your attempt with the model answer and assess how much of the answer you achieved.

## Stage 3: Final pre-exam revision

We recommend that you **attempt at least one two hour mock examination** containing a set of previously unseen exam standard questions.

Attempt the mock CBA online in timed, closed book conditions to simulate the real exam experience.

# Section 1

# PRACTICE QUESTIONS

## PRACTICE PAPER 1

TOY SHOP

### THE SITUATION

This assignment is based on an existing business, Toy Shop, a small manufacturer who has recently set up in business selling:

- Boxed Games
- Computer games
- Jigsaws

The owner of the business is James Free who operates as a sole trader.

At the start of the business James operated a manual bookkeeping system but has now decided that from 1st May 20XX the accounting system will become computerised.

You can assume that all documentation has been checked and authorised by James Free.

Some nominal ledger accounts have already been allocated suitable account codes. **You may need to amend or create other account codes.**

Set the company's Financial Year to start in May of the current year.

Their company details are:-

Toy Shop

64 Long Lane

Langhorne

North Yorkshire

YO21 3EJ

Tel: 01234 567891

You are employed as an accounting technician.

The business is registered for VAT. The rate of VAT charged on all goods and services sold by Toy Shops is 20%. VAT registration number 123456789.

## TASK 1

Refer to the customer listing below and set up customer records to open Sales Ledger accounts for each customer.

| Customer account code | Customer name, address and contact details | Customer account details | |
| --- | --- | --- | --- |
| BB01 | Busy Bee Toys<br>832 High Street<br>Oxford<br>OX2 3WG | Credit limit:<br>Payment Terms:<br>Opening Balance:<br>(relates to invoice 021 dated 12th Apr) | £4000<br>30 days<br>£349.20 |
| FF02 | Forming Fun<br>21 Newton Quay<br>Knott Mill<br>Manchester M6 3RJ | Credit limit:<br>Payment Terms:<br>Opening Balance:<br>(relates to invoice 035 dated 8th Apr ) | £4000<br>30 days<br>£99.60 |
| SM03 | Space Models<br>13 Central Street<br>Perth<br>Scotland<br>SC4 8RQ | Credit limit:<br>Payment Terms:<br>Opening Balance:<br>(relates to invoice 093 dated 10th Apr) | £3000<br>30 days<br>£1195.20 |
| TP04 | Teddy T's Party<br>3 Paradise Street<br>Wokingham<br>WO4 6QP | Credit limit:<br>Payment Terms:<br>Opening Balance:<br>(relates to invoice 1003 dated 17th Apr) | £7000<br>30 days<br>£579.60 |

## TASK 2

Refer to the supplier listing below and set up supplier records to open Purchase Ledger accounts for each supplier.

| Supplier account code | Supplier name, address and contact details | Supplier account details | |
| --- | --- | --- | --- |
| PL01 | Abacus C & C<br>Unit 31<br>Kitts Industrial Estate<br>St Helens<br>Lancs | Credit limit:<br>Payment Terms:<br>Opening Balance:<br>(relates to invoice B/1874 dated 2nd Apr) | £5500<br>30 days<br>£369.60 |
| PL02 | Compugames Ltd<br>6 Jury Road<br>Dublin<br>Eire | Credit limit:<br>Payment Terms:<br>Opening Balance:<br>(relates to invoice 1087 dated 11th Apr) | £4000<br>30 days<br>£511.20 |
| PL03 | Space Models<br>13 Central Street<br>Perth<br>Scotland | Credit limit:<br>Payment Terms:<br>Opening Balance:<br>(relates to invoice F-0193 dated 18th Apr) | £2000<br>30 days<br>£306 |
| PL04 | Toys Unlimited<br>95 Cuscaden Road<br>Edinburgh<br>Scotland | Credit limit:<br>Payment Terms:<br>Opening Balance:<br>(relates to invoice W/032 dated 18th Apr) | £2000<br>30 days<br>£970.80 |

## TASK 3.1

Refer to the list of General ledger balances below. Enter the opening balances onto the computerised accounting system, making sure you select/create/amend the appropriate general ledger account codes.

List of general ledger balances as at the **1st May**

| Account name | DR | CR |
|---|---|---|
| | £ | £ |
| Furniture and fixtures | 5800.00 | |
| Motor Vehicles | 3000.00 | |
| Bank | 4225.00 | |
| Petty Cash | 300.00 | |
| Sales Ledger Control Account * | 2223.60 | |
| Purchase Ledger Control Account * | | 2157.60 |
| VAT on sales | | 543.00 |
| VAT on purchases | 109.00 | |
| Capital | | 20000.00 |
| Drawings | 355.00 | |
| Sales – Computer Games | | 6080.00 |
| Sales – Jigsaws | | 700.00 |
| Sales – Boxed Games | | 1967.00 |
| Purchases – Computer Games | 8000.00 | |
| Purchases – Jigsaws | 3200.00 | |
| Purchases – Boxed Games | 2465.00 | |
| Office Stationery | 53.00 | |
| Electricity | 167.00 | |
| Rent and Rates | 1550.00 | |
| ***Note** <br> You do not need to enter these figures as you have already entered opening balances for customers and suppliers | | |

## TASK 3.2

Transfer £500 from the bank current account to the bank deposit account. Enter this on the computerised accounting system using reference TRANS01 dated 1st May.

## TASK 3.3

Produce the following reports and **identify and correct any errors**:

- Customer Address List
- Supplier Address List
- Trial Balance Report

## TASK 4

Enter the following sales invoices and credit note onto the computerised accounting system.

---

Toy Shops
64 Long Lane
Langhorne
North Yorkshire
YO21 3EJ

Telephone: 0121 765 3213
Email: jp@toyshops.co.uk

Sales Invoice No 2021

Date: 4th May 20XX

---

Busy Bee Toys
832 High Street
Oxford
OX2 3WG

| Description | £ |
|---|---|
| Computer Games | 2585.00 |
| | |
| VAT @ 20.00% | 517.00 |
| Total for payment | 3102.00 |

Terms 30 days

---

Toy Shops
64 Long Lane
Langhorne
North Yorkshire
YO21 3EJ

Telephone: 0121 765 3213
Email: jp@toyshops.co.uk

Sales Invoice No 2022

Date: 4th May 20XX

---

Forming Fun
21 Newton Quay
Knott Mill
Manchester
M6 3RJ

| Description | £ |
|---|---|
| Boxed Games | 500.00 |
| VAT @ 20.00% | 100.00 |
| Total for payment | 600.00 |

Terms 30 days

---

Toy Shops
64 Long Lane
Langhorne
North Yorkshire
YO21 3EJ

Telephone: 0121 765 3213
Email: jp@toyshops.co.uk

Sales Invoice No 2023

Date: 6th May 20XX

Teddy T's Party
3 Paradise Street
Wokingham
WO4 6QP

| Description | £ |
|---|---|
| Computer games | 5000.00 |
| | |
| VAT @ 20.00% | 1000.00 |
| Total for payment | 6000.00 |

Terms 30 days

Toy Shops
64 Long Lane
Langhorne
North Yorkshire
YO21 3EJ

Telephone: 0121 765 3213
Email: jp@toyshops.co.uk

Credit Note No CN101

Date: 13th May 20XX

Teddy T's Party
3 Paradise Street
Wokingham
WO4 6QP

| **Description** | £ |
|---|---|
| Return faulty Computer games | 320.00 |
| VAT @ 20.00% | 64.00 |
| Total credit | 384.00 |

## TASK 5.1

Enter the following purchases invoices onto the computer system.

| Date | A/C No. | Invoice Ref | Gross | Vat | Net | Computer games | Jigsaws | Boxed Games |
|------|---------|-------------|-------|-----|-----|----------------|---------|-------------|
| 3rd May | PL01 | B/989 | 540.00 | 90.00 | 450.00 | 450.00 | | |
| 5th May | PL02 | 145215 | 600.00 | 100.00 | 500.00 | | | 500.00 |
| 10th May | PL03 | C-32632 | 1200.00 | 200.00 | 1000.00 | 1000.00 | | |
| 10th May | PL04 | 12421 | 18.00 | 0.00 | 18.00 | | 18.00 | |

## TASK 5.2

Enter the following purchase credit note onto the computer system.

| Date | Supplier | N/C | Credit Note Ref | Description | Details |
|------|----------|-----|-----------------|-------------|---------|
| 15th May | Compugames | 5000 | 11245 | Computer Games | £88.00 Plus tax |

## TASK 6

The following remittance advices were received from customers. Enter the receipts onto the computerised accounting system.

---

**Busy Bee Toys**

**Remittance Advice**

To: Toy Shop

Date: 17 May 20XX

A cheque for £349.20 (number 100322) is attached in payment of invoice no 021.

---

**Forming Fun**

**Remittance Advice**

To: Toy Shop

Date: 17 May 20XX

A cheque for £99.60 (number 267543) is attached in payment of invoice 035.

---

| | |
|---|---|
| **Teddy T's Party** | |
| **BACS Remittance Advice** | |

To: Toy Shop

Date: 26 May 20XX

An amount of £195.60 has been paid directly into your bank account in payment of invoice 1003, including credit note CN101.

## TASK 7

The following cheque payments were sent to suppliers; enter the payments on the accounts system. **Produce the relevant remittance advices.**

| Date | Cheque No | Supplier | Amount | Details |
|---|---|---|---|---|
| 22nd May | 101333 | Abacus C & C | 369.60 | Inv B/1874 |
| 22nd May | 101334 | Compugames | 1005.60 | Settle account in full. |

## TASK 8

Refer to the following cash sales and enter receipts into the computer. Use the bank current account for this transaction and enter 'cash sales' as the reference.

| Date | Receipt Type | Gross | VAT | NET | Nominal code |
|---|---|---|---|---|---|
| 13th May | Cash sale | 1,200.00 | 200.00 | 1,000.00 | 4000 |
| 13th May | Cash sale | 2,879.40 | 479.90 | 2,399.50 | 4001 |
| 20th May | Cash sale | 995.00 | 0.00 | 995.00 | 4000 |

## TASK 9

Enter the following petty cash payments onto the computerised accounting system.

| **Petty Cash Voucher** | | **Petty Cash Voucher** | |
|---|---|---|---|
| **Date:** | 20.05.XX | **Date:** | 21.05.XX |
| **Voucher No:** | 012 | **Voucher No:** | 013 |
| **Details** | £ | **Details** | £ |
| Subscriptions | 32.00 | Refreshments | 10.40 |
| (no Vat) | | VAT | 2.08 |
| | | Total | 12.48 |
| **Authorised By;** | *James Free* | **Authorised By;** | *James Free* |
| Receipt attached | | Receipt attached | |

## TASK 10

Enter the following journal on the computerised accounting system.

| Reference: JNL02 | | | |
|---|---|---|---|
| Date | Account Name & Code | Dr | Cr |
| 25th May | Drawings | 2000.00 | |
| | Bank | | 2000.00 |
| Being the transfer of cash for James Free's personal use. | | | |

## TASK 11

Produce the following reports:

(a)     Trial Balance Report for May (including opening balances)

(b)     Sales Day Book

(c)     Sales Returns Day Book

(d)     Purchase Day Book

(e)     Customer Activity Report

(f)     Supplier Activity Report

(g)     Aged Creditors Report (Detailed)

(h)     Aged Debtors Report (Detailed)

## TASK 12

Refer to the following email below from James Free.

| E-Mail |
|---|
| **From:**     James Free |
| **To:**     Accounts Technician |
| **Date:**     19th May 20XX |
| **Subject:** |

Hello

A credit customer Forming Fun has moved premises. Their new address is as follows:

100 Aventi Way

St Albans

Hertfordshire

AL2 4PM

Please ensure that this is updated on the computerised accounts system.

Thanks

James

**Create a screen shot** of the customer's record with the new address and save it as a 'Word' document.

## TASK 13

The sum of £502.00 has been incorrectly posted to the rent account instead of the electricity account in error. Process the following journal to correct this using reference JNL03. Use 31st May for the transaction.

| Reference: JNL03 | | | |
|---|---|---|---|
| Date | Account Name & Code | Dr | Cr |
| 31st May | Electricity | 502.00 | |
| | Rent & Rates | | 502.00 |

Being the transfer of cash which was incorrectly posted to Rent instead of Electricity.

## TASK 14

The following cheque payments were sent to suppliers; enter the payments on the accounts system and **produce the relevant remittance advices**.

| Date | Supplier | Cheque No | Details | Amount |
|---|---|---|---|---|
| 28th May | Space Models | 101335 | Payment of opening balance | 306.00 |
| 28th May | Toys Unlimited | 101336 | Part payment invoice W/032 | 450.00 |
| 28th May | Abacus C & C | BACS | Payment of invoice B/989 | 540.00 |

## TASK 15

The following payments were received from customers; enter the receipts on the accounts system, dated 29 May 20XX.

| Customer | Cheque No | Details | Amount (£) |
|---|---|---|---|
| Busy Bee | 104662 | Invoice 2021 | 3102.00 |
| Forming Fun | 828100 | Part payment invoice 2022 | 400.00 |
| Teddy T's Party | 672522 | Payment of invoice 2023 | 6000.00 |

## TASK 16

On 14th May a member of staff buys Computer Games paying you £264.00 in Cash. This is inclusive of 20% VAT. Enter this in the bank current account and use reference CSH41 for this transaction.

## TASK 17

On 19th May, you sold a 'Jigsaw' to a customer and they paid £45.00 (Zero rated VAT) debit card. Enter this in the bank current account and use reference 'Debit Card' for this transaction.

## TASK 18

On the 5th May you are asked to set up a monthly recurring payment for a Direct Debit. It is to pay Insurance for £100.00 (Exempt VAT) for a period of 12 months commencing on 31st May. There is no VAT on this transaction. Select/create/amend any ledger accounts. The Insurance is payable to Galloway Union. Provide evidence by taking a screen shot and saving it as a 'Word' document. Ensure you process this month's transaction.

## TASK 19

You are asked to ensure that the petty cash account float is restored to a balance of £300.00 by bank transfer (dated 31st May). Enter this transaction onto the computerised system and use reference CSH25.

## TASK 20

Toy Shop has been granted a bank loan for £10,000.00 and it has been received in to the bank current account on 31 May 20XX. Process the following journal to record this transaction (use ref JNL04).

| Reference: JNL04 | | | |
|---|---|---|---|
| Date | Account Name & Code | Dr | Cr |
| 31st May | Bank Current Account | 10000.00 | |
| | Loan Account | | 10000.00 |

Being the proceeds received for a new loan.

**TASK 21**

You are given the following bank statement and are asked to produce a bank reconciliation as at 31st May, processing any adjustments that may be necessary.

**Friendly Bank plc**

201 Main Road

Rochester

Kent

ME15 9JP

Toy Shop

64 Long Lane

Langthorne

North Yorkshire

YO21 3EJ

31st May 20XX

Statement no: 0003

Account number: 00678432

**Statement of Account**

| Date: May 20XX | Details | Paid out £ | Paid in £ | Balance £ |
|---|---|---|---|---|
| 1 May | Opening balance | | | 4225.00C |
| 1 May | Transfer | 500.00 | | 3725.00C |
| 13 May | Counter credit | | 1200.00 | 4925.00C |
| 13 May | Counter credit | | 2879.40 | 7804.40C |
| 14 May | Counter credit | | 264.00 | 8068.40C |
| 17 May | Counter credit | | 349.20 | 8417.60C |
| 17 May | Counter credit | | 99.60 | 8517.20C |
| 19 May | Debit Card | | 45.00 | 8562.20C |
| 20 May | Counter credit | | 995.00 | 9557.20C |
| 22 May | Cheque 101333 | 369.60 | | 9187.60C |
| 23 May | Cheque 101334 | 1005.60 | | 8182.00C |
| 25 May | Counter debit Ref: JNL 02 | 2000.00 | | 6182.00C |
| 26 May | BACS: Teddy's T Party | | 195.60 | 6377.60C |
| 28 May | Cheque 101336 | 450.00 | | 5927.60C |
| 29 May | Counter credit | | 3102.00 | 9029.60C |
| 29 May | Counter credit | | 6000.00 | 15029.60C |
| 29 May | Counter credit | | 400.00 | 15429.60C |
| 30 May | BACS payment | 540.00 | | 14889.60C |
| 31 May | Transfer | 44.48 | | 14845.12C |
| 31 May | Direct Debit – Galloway Union | 100.00 | | 14745.12C |
| 31 May | Bank charges | 101.32 | | 14643.80C |
| 31 May | Loan | | 10000.00 | 24643.80C |
| | D = Debit C = Credit | | | |

**TASK 22**

Produce the following reports

(a)     Customer Activity (detailed) Report

(b)     Supplier Activity (detailed) Report

(c)     Period Trial Balance for the month of May (including opening balances)

(d)     Audit Trail for May (detailed – transactions only including bank reconciled & opening balances)

(e)     Aged Debtors (summary)

# PRACTICE PAPER 2

## CRAZY HAIR

### THE SITUATION

This assignment is based on a new business, Crazy Hair, a small business recently set up to selling hair products.

The owner of the business is Nina Birk who operates as a sole trader.

At the start of the business Nina operated a manual bookkeeping system but has now decided that from 1st May 20XX the accounting system will become computerised.

You can assume that all documentation has been checked and authorised by Nina Birk.

Some nominal ledger accounts have already been allocated suitable account codes. **You may need to amend or create other account codes.**

Crazy Hair's financial year starts in May of the current year.

Their company details are:-

Crazy Hair

34 Clapham Road

Clapham

London

SE3 2HR

Tel: 01234 567891

You are employed as an accounting technician.

The business is registered for VAT. The rate of VAT charged on all goods and services sold by Crazy Hair is 20%. VAT registration number 123456789.

## TASK 1

Refer to the customer listing below and set up customer records to open Sales Ledger accounts for each customer.

| Customer account code | Customer name, address and contact details | Customer account details | | |
|---|---|---|---|---|
| 104 | Alfred Images<br>Masuki Offices<br>PO Box 5684<br>Birmingham  B23 4RD | Credit limit:<br>Payment Terms:<br>Opening Balance:<br>(relates to invoice 3352 dated 2nd April) | £8000<br>30 days<br>£1809.60 | |
| 110 | Figgaro<br>Beta Studio<br>34 Knightsbridge Way<br>Morden  SE23 4KA | Credit limit:<br>Payment Terms:<br>Opening Balance:<br>(relates to invoice 2856 dated 10th April) | £6500<br>30 days<br>£3880.80 | |
| 118 | Blades<br>Alpha Studio<br>45 Key West<br>London  SE1 0JF | Credit limit:<br>Payment Terms:<br>Opening Balance:<br>(relates to invoice 3345 dated 18th April) | £6100<br>30 days<br>£2144.40 | |
| 122 | Hair Studio<br>Framlington Court<br>Lee<br>London  SE4 7YH | Credit limit:<br>Payment Terms:<br>Opening Balance:<br>(relates to invoice 3098 dated 12th April) | £5000<br>30 days<br>£681.60 | |
| 138 | Ribbons & Curls<br>PO Box 1120<br>Canning Town<br>London  TN2 2EB | Credit limit:<br>Payment Terms:<br>Opening Balance:<br>(relates to invoice 3123 dated 12th April) | £5000<br>30 days<br>£391.20 | |

**TASK 2**

Refer to the supplier listing below and set up supplier records to open Purchase Ledger accounts for each supplier.

| Supplier account code | Supplier name, address and contact details | Supplier account details | |
|---|---|---|---|
| 1134 | Avada Cash & Carry<br>32 Surrey Quay<br>Isle of Dogs<br>E12 3NW | Credit limit:<br>Payment Terms:<br>Opening Balance:<br>(relates to invoice C/251 dated 22nd April) | £5500<br>30 days<br>£4454.40 |
| 1138 | Straightside Supplies<br>Havering Place<br>Holborn<br>London<br>WC1 2PP | Credit limit:<br>Payment Terms:<br>Opening Balance:<br>(relates to invoice 9140 dated 11th April) | £12000<br>30 days<br>£1839.60 |
| 1165 | Hair Supplies<br>43 St Helens Way<br>London<br>SE7 3RF | Credit limit:<br>Payment Terms:<br>Opening Balance:<br>(relates to invoice 0028 dated 11th April) | £4000<br>30 days<br>£818.40 |
| 1185 | Wig Specialists<br>Retro Square<br>32 Wigmore Road<br>London<br>EC1V 3SG | Credit limit:<br>Payment Terms:<br>Opening Balance:<br>(relates to invoice S653 dated 18th April) | £5000<br>30 days<br>£102.00 |

## TASK 3.1

Refer to the list of General ledger balances below. Enter the opening balances into the computer, making sure you select/create/amend the appropriate general ledger account codes.

List of general ledger balances as at the **1st May**

| Account name | £ | £ |
|---|---|---|
| Motor Vehicle | 24000.00 | |
| Furniture and Fixtures | 31000.00 | |
| Bank | 54210.81 | |
| Petty Cash | 200.00 | |
| Sales Ledger Control Account * | 8907.60 | |
| Purchase Ledger Control Account* | | 7214.40 |
| VAT on Sales | | 5550.00 |
| VAT on Purchases | 1507.94 | |
| Capital | | 165000.00 |
| Drawings | 5000.00 | |
| Sales – Brushes | | 345.00 |
| Sales – Combs | | 187.00 |
| Sales – Colours | | 3801.45 |
| Sales – Hairdryers | | 758.00 |
| Sales – Wigs | | 5600.00 |
| Cash Sales | | 617.50 |
| Purchases – Brushes | 873.00 | |
| Purchases – Combs | 50.00 | |
| Purchases – Colour | 4200.00 | |
| Purchases – Hairdryers | 6310.00 | |
| Purchases – Wigs | 52814.00 | |
| **\*Note**<br><br>You do not need to enter these figures as you have already entered opening balances for customers and suppliers. | | |

## TASK 3.2

Produce the following reports and **identify and correct any errors**:

(a)     Customer Address List

(b)     Supplier Address List

(c)     Trial Balance

**TASK 4**

Enter the following sales invoices onto the computer.

Crazy Hair
34 Clapham Road
Clapham
London
SE3 2HR

Account No: 138
Invoice No: 3353

Date: 12 May 20XX

Ribbons & Curls
PO Box 1120
Canning Town
London
TN2 2EB

| Quantity | Description | Unit Price | Net Cost | Tax | Gross | Nominal code |
|----------|-------------|------------|----------|-------|--------|--------------|
| 10 | Colours | 14.10 | 141.00 | 28.20 | 169.20 | 4002 |

Terms 30 days

Crazy Hair
34 Clapham Road
Clapham
London
SE3 2HR

Account No: 104
Invoice No: 3354

Date: 12 May 20XX

Alfred Images
Masuki Offices
PO Box 5684
Birmingham
B23 4RD

| Quantity | Description | Unit Price | Net Cost | Tax | Gross | Nominal code |
|----------|-------------|------------|----------|--------|--------|--------------|
| 50 | Brushes | 11.62 | 581.00 | 116.20 | 697.20 | 4000 |

Terms 30 days

Crazy Hair
34 Clapham Road
Clapham
London
SE3 2HR

Account No: 110
Invoice No: 3355

Date: 13th May 20XX

Figgaro
Beta Studio
34 Knightsbridge Way
Morden
SE23 4KA

| Quantity | Description | Unit Price | Net Cost | Tax | Gross | Nominal code |
|---|---|---|---|---|---|---|
| 12 | Hairdryers | 55.00 | 660.00 | 132.00 | 792.00 | 4003 |

Terms 30 days

Crazy Hair
34 Clapham Road
Clapham
London
SE3 2HR

Account No: 118
Invoice No:  3356

Date:  15th May 20XX

Blades
Alpha Studio
45 Key West
London
SE1 0JF

| Quantity | Description | Unit Price | Net Cost | Tax | Gross | Nominal code |
|---|---|---|---|---|---|---|
| 8 | Wigs | 210.72 | 1685.76 | 337.15 | 2022.91 | 4004 |
| 3 | Hairdryers | 67.80 | 203.40 | 40.68 | 244.08 | 4003 |

Terms 30 days

Crazy Hair
34 Clapham Road
Clapham
London
SE3 2HR

Account No: 122
Invoice No: 3357

Date: 18 May 20XX

Hair Studio
Framlington Court
Lee
London
SE4 7YH

| Quantity | Description | Unit Price | Net Cost | Tax | Gross | Nominal code |
|---|---|---|---|---|---|---|
| 12 | Brushes | 26.40 | 316.80 | 63.36 | 380.16 | 4000 |
| 4 | Wigs | 220.48 | 881.92 | 176.38 | 1058.30 | 4004 |
| 16 | Colours | 14.40 | 230.40 | 46.08 | 276.48 | 4002 |

Terms 30 days

## TASK 5

On 25th May you send a credit note (CN23) to Alfred Images (Account No 104) for brushes.

The total is £67.20 which includes tax.

## TASK 6

Enter the purchases invoices into the computer.

| Date | A/C No. | Invoice Ref | Description | Nominal Code | Net | Vat | Gross |
|---|---|---|---|---|---|---|---|
| 11 May | 1138 | 3362 | Brushes | 5000 | 191.60 | 38.32 | 229.92 |
| 11 May | 1134 | C/910 | Colours | 5002 | 954.00 | 190.80 | 1144.80 |
| 13 May | 1165 | 0814 | Hairdryers | 5003 | 178.56 | 0.00 | 178.56 |
| 14 May | 1185 | S1198 | Wigs | 5004 | 3393.60 | 678.72 | 4072.32 |

## TASK 7

Enter the following purchase credit note onto the computer system.

| Date | A/C No | Supplier | N/C | Credit Note Ref | Amount |
|---|---|---|---|---|---|
| 18 May | 1185 | Wigs Specialist | 5004 | C3223 | 123.24 Including Vat |

## TASK 8

The following payments were received from customers; enter the receipts on the accounts system.

| Date | Receipt type | Customer | Amount | Details |
|------|-------------|----------|--------|---------|
| 20 May | Cheque No: 183001 | Alfred Images | 1809.60 | Payment for invoice 3352 |
| 21 May | Cheque No: 654255 | Blades | 2144.40 | Payment for invoice 3345 |
| 21 May | BACS | Figgaro | 3880.80 | Payment for invoice 2856 |
| 21 May | Cheque No: 452221 | Hair Studio | 681.60 | Payment for invoice 3098 |

## TASK 9

The following cheque payments were sent to suppliers; enter the payments on the accounts system dated 31st May and **produce the relevant remittance advices**.

| Supplier | Cheque No: | Amount | Details |
|----------|-----------|--------|---------|
| Wigs Specialist | 163455 | £102.00 | Payment for invoice S653 |
| Avada Cash & Carry | 163456 | £4454.40 | Payment for invoice C/251 |
| Hair Supplies | 163457 | £818.40 | Payment for invoice 0028 |

## TASK 10

Enter the following petty cash payments into the computer. Check the nominal codes before entering the payments and select/create/amend any ledger accounts where necessary.

| Date | Ref | Nominal Code | Net | VAT | Gross |
|------|-----|-------------|-----|-----|-------|
| 19 May | CSH 86 | 7400 | 33.60 | 6.72 | 40.32 |
| 20 May | CSH 87 | 7500 | 4.51 | 0.00 | 4.51 |

## TASK 11

On the 20th May, a member of staff purchases a 'Brush' from you and pays Crazy Hair a total of £21.00 in cash. This is inclusive of VAT of £3.50. Enter this in the bank current account and use reference 1001 for this transaction.

## TASK 12

Produce the following reports:

(a)   Trial Balance Report

(b)   Sales Day Book

(c)   Sales Returns Day Book

(d)   Purchase Day Book

(e)   Customer Activity Report

(f)   Supplier Activity Report

(g)   Aged Creditors Report (summary)

(h)   Aged Debtors Report (summary)

## TASK 13

Enter the following journal

<table>
<tr><td colspan="4" style="text-align:center">Ref : JH12</td></tr>
<tr><td>Date</td><td>Account Name & Code</td><td>Dr</td><td>Cr</td></tr>
<tr><td>24 May</td><td>Drawings</td><td>440.00</td><td></td></tr>
<tr><td></td><td>Bank</td><td></td><td>440.00</td></tr>
</table>

Being the transfer of cash for personal use.

## TASK 14

(a)    Refer to the following email below from Frances Williams

| E-Mail |
| --- |
| From: Frances Williams |
| Date: 19th May 20XX |
| Subject: Customer change of address |
| |
| Hello |
| |
| A credit customer Ribbons and Curls has moved premises. New address as follows: |
| 122 Devonshire Road |
| Cranbrook |
| London |
| SE1 2AB |
| Please ensure that this is updated on the computerised accounts system. |
| |
| Thanks |
| Frances |

(b)    **Create a screen shot** of the customer's record showing the change of address and save it as a 'Word' document. Use a suitable file name to save the document.

## TASK 15

On 31st May you transfer £30.52 from the Bank account to the petty cash account. Use reference TRF01.

## TASK 16

You are given the following bank statement and are asked to produce a bank reconciliation at 31st May, processing any adjustments that may be necessary. Ensure that the direct debit for Coopers Union is coded to Premises Insurance costs. Check the nominal codes list and select/create/amend any ledger accounts where necessary. There is no VAT applicable on both direct debits.

**Nice Bank plc**
201 Main Road
Rochester
Kent
ME15 9JP

Crazy Hair
34 Clapham Road
London
SE3 2HR

31st May 20XX

Statement no: 0012

Account number: 32543211

**Statement of Account**

| Date: May 20XX | Details | Paid out £ | Paid in £ | Balance £ |
|---|---|---|---|---|
| 01 May | Opening balance | | | 54210.81C |
| 14 May | Counter credit | | 1809.60 | 56020.41C |
| 20 May | Counter credit | | 2144.40 | 58164.81C |
| 20 May | BACS | | 3880.80 | 62045.61C |
| 20 May | Counter credit | | 681.60 | 62727.21C |
| 20 May | Counter credit | | 21.00 | 62748.21C |
| 24 May | Counter Debit | 440.00 | | 62308.21C |
| 24 May | Direct Debit – Coopers Union | 168.00 | | 62140.11C |
| 24 May | Counter Debit | 30.52 | | 62109.69C |
| 31 May | Direct Debit – Electricity | 66.94 | | 62042.75C |
| 31 May | Bank Charges | 27.11 | | 62015.64C |
| | D = Debit C = Credit | | | |

## TASK 17

Produce the following reports

(a)    Customer Address List

(b)    Customer Activity

(c)    Supplier Activity

(d)    Trial Balance for the month of May (include opening balances)

(e)    Audit Trail for May only (Detailed – including opening balances)

(f)    Aged Creditors (summary)

(g)    Aged Debtors (summary)

(h)    Nominal Ledger Activity Report for the following accounts

1.1.1. Bank Current Account

1.1.2. Petty Cash Account

# PRACTICE PAPER 3

## SHOES 4U

### THE SITUATION

This assignment is based on an existing organisation, Shoes 4U, a small business selling ladies and men's shoes.

The owner of the business is Dennis Cope who operates as a sole trader.

At the start of the business Dennis operated a manual bookkeeping system but has now decided that from 1st June 20XX the accounting system will become computerised.

You can assume that all documentation has been checked by Dennis Cope.

Some nominal ledger accounts have already been allocated suitable account codes. **You may need to amend or create other account codes.**

Shoes 4U's financial year starts in June of the current year.

Their company details are:-

Shoes 4U

85 Barrington Close

Carlisle

Cumbria

C41 3ED

Tel: 01234 567891

You are employed as an accounting technician.

The business is registered for VAT. The rate of VAT charged on all goods and services sold by Shoes 4U is 20%. VAT registration number 123456789.

## TASK 1

Refer to the customer listing below and set up customer records to open Sales Ledger accounts for each customer.

| Customer account code | Customer name, address and contact details | Customer account details |
|---|---|---|
| SL186 | Beckers Gate Ltd<br>Butchergate<br>Carlisle<br>Cumbria  C41 1SG | Credit limit:          £5000<br>Payment Terms:     30 days<br>Opening Balance:  £4811.88<br>(relates to invoice 1613 dated 22nd May) |
| SL213 | Eaton Bowls Club<br>Seaton Street<br>St Neots<br>Cambs  PE19 8EF | Credit limit:          £3000<br>Payment Terms:     30 days<br>Opening Balance:   £961.98<br>(relates to invoice 1582 dated 10th May) |
| SL302 | Jones Footwear<br>Scotby Village<br>Carlisle<br>Cumbria  C44 8BP | Credit limit:          £6000<br>Payment Terms:     30 days<br>Opening Balance:  £3828.75<br>(relates to invoice 1596 dated 28th May) |
| SL307 | Dickens Ladies Footwear<br>17 Royal Square<br>Bleachfield<br>North Yorkshire  YO87 9AD | Credit limit:          £11000<br>Payment Terms:     30 days<br>Opening Balance:   £783.66<br>(relates to invoice 1601 dated 21st May) |

## TASK 2

Refer to the supplier listing below and set up supplier records to open Purchase Ledger accounts for each supplier.

| Supplier account code | Supplier name, address and contact details | Supplier account details |
|---|---|---|
| PL112 | Bootsy & Smudge Ltd<br>Factory Road<br>Stilton<br>Cambs  PE7 3RP | Credit limit:          £4000<br>Payment Terms:        30 days<br>Opening Balance:      £2881.26<br>(relates to invoice B/468 dated 22nd May) |
| PL168 | Briggsthorpe Boots<br>Long Buckby Wharf<br>Long Buckby<br>Northampton  NN4 9UW | Credit limit:          £50000<br>Payment Terms:        30 days<br>Opening Balance:      £43200.00<br>(relates to invoice 0001087 dated 18th May) |
| PL172 | Gallows Fashion<br>18 The Crescent<br>Pickford<br>Cambs  PE7 8QV | Credit limit:          £2000<br>Payment Terms:        30 days<br>Opening Balance:      £400.00<br>(relates to invoice G-01239 dated 16th May) |
| PL173 | Dickens Ladies Footwear<br>17 Royal Square<br>Bleachfield<br>North Yorkshire<br>YO87 9AD | Credit limit:          £2000<br>Payment Terms:        30 days<br>Opening Balance:      £567.00<br>(relates to invoice 06345 dated 16th May) |

**TASK 3.1**

Refer to the list of General ledger balances below. Enter the opening balances into the computer, making sure you select/create/amend the appropriate general ledger account codes.

List of general ledger balances as at the 1st June

| Account name | £ | £ |
|---|---|---|
| Freehold Property | 72000.00 | |
| Motor Vehicles | 7500.00 | |
| Furniture and Fixtures | 9000.00 | |
| Bank | 19363.00 | |
| Petty Cash | 200.00 | |
| Sales Ledger Control * | 10386.27 | |
| Purchase Ledger Control * | | 47048.26 |
| VAT on Sales | | 3402.35 |
| VAT on Purchases | 1130.00 | |
| Capital | | 30000.00 |
| Drawings | 600.00 | |
| Sales – Men's Footwear | | 79320.00 |
| Sales – Ladies Footwear | | 43210.00 |
| Cash Sales | | 6798.00 |
| Purchases – Men's Footwear | 55432.00 | |
| Purchases – Ladies Footwear | 23410.00 | |
| Advertising | 7231.00 | |
| Telephone | 866.00 | |
| Rent | 1263.00 | |
| Electricity | 567.34 | |
| Office Stationery | 830.00 | |
| *Note* <br> You do not need to enter these figures as you have already entered opening balances for customers and suppliers | | |

**TASK 3.2**

Transfer £5000 from the bank current account to the bank deposit account, dated 1st June. Use TRF01 as the reference.

**TASK 3.3**

Produce the following reports and identify and correct any errors:

(a)     Customer Address list

(b)     Supplier Address List

(c)     Period Trial Balance Report

**TASK 4**

Enter the following sales invoices and credit notes on to the computer.

---

**Shoes 4u**
85 Barrington Close
Carlisle
Cumbria
C41 3ED

Sales Invoice No: 1622
Date: 4th June 20XX

---

Becker Gate Ltd
Butchergate
Carlisle
Cumbria
C41 1SG

| Description | £ |
|---|---|
| Men's Footwear | 450.00 |
| | |
| VAT @ 20.00% | 90.00 |
| Total for payment | 540.00 |

Terms 30 days

---

**Shoes 4u**
85 Barrington Close
Carlisle
Cumbria
C41 3ED

Sales Invoice No: 1623
Date: 6th June 20XX

---

Eaton Bowls Club
Seaton Street
St Neots
Cambs
PE19 8EF

| Description | £ |
|---|---|
| Men's Footwear | 1385.00 |
| | |
| VAT @ 20.00% | 277.00 |
| Total for payment | 1662.00 |

Terms 30 days

---

**Shoes 4u**
85 Barrington Close
Carlisle
Cumbria
C41 3ED

Sales Invoice No: 1624
Date: 14th June 20XX

Dickens Ladies Footwear
17 Royal Square
Bleachfield
North Yorkshire
YO87 9AD

| Description | £ |
|---|---|
| Men's Footwear | 450.00 |
| Ladies Footwear | 1850.00 |
| | |
| VAT @ 20.00% | 460.00 |
| Total for payment | 2760.00 |

Terms 30 days

**Shoes 4u**
85 Barrington Close
Carlisle
Cumbria
C41 3ED

Sales Invoice No: 1625
Date: 17th June 20XX

Jones Footwear
Scotby Village
Carlisle
Cumbria
C44 8BP

| Description | £ |
|---|---|
| Ladies Footwear | 1175.75 |
| | |
| VAT @ 20.00% | 235.15 |
| Total for payment | 1410.90 |

Terms 30 days

```
                         Shoes 4u
                    85 Barrington Close
                         Carlisle
                         Cumbria
                         C41 3ED
```

Credit Note No: CR10
Date: 8th June 20XX

---

Dickens Ladies Footwear

17 Royal Square

Bleachfield

North Yorkshire

YO87 9AD

| Description | £ |
|---|---|
| Returned Ladies Footwear – Damage in transit | 235.00 |
| | |
| VAT @ 20.00% | 47.00 |
| Total for payment | 282.00 |

Terms 30 days

## TASK 5

Enter supplier invoices into the computer.

| Date | Description | N/C | Invoice Ref | Net | Vat | Gross |
|---|---|---|---|---|---|---|
| 2 June | Bootsy & Smudge Ltd | 5001 | B/752 | 300.00 | 60.00 | 360.00 |
| 10 June | Briggsthorpe Boots | 5000 | 12350 | 2500.00 | 500.00 | 3000.00 |
| 12 June | Gallows Fashion | 5000 | G-2285 | 2500.00 | 500.00 | 3000.00 |
| 13 June | Bootsy & Smudge Ltd | 5001 | B/753 | 200.00 | 40.00 | 240.00 |

## TASK 6

The following payments were received from customers; enter the receipts on the accounts system.

| Date | A/c No | Customer | Cheque No | Details | Amount £ |
|---|---|---|---|---|---|
| 11 June | SL186 | Beckers Gate Ltd | 199846 | Payment for invoice 1613 | 4811.88 |
| 14 June | SL213 | Eaton Bowls Club | 107654 | Payment for invoice 1582 | 961.98 |
| 14 June | SL302 | Jones Footwear | 244536 | Payment for invoice 1596 | 3828.75 |

## TASK 7

The following cheque payments were sent to suppliers; enter the payments on the accounts system and **raise the relevant remittance advices**.

| Date | A/c No | Supplier | Cheque No | Details | Amount £ |
|------|--------|----------|-----------|---------|----------|
| 18 June | PL172 | Gallows Fashion | 109887 | Payment for invoice G-01239 | 400.00 |
| 18 June | PL168 | Briggsthorpe Boots | 109888 | Part Payment for invoice 0001087 | 23300.00 |

## TASK 8.1

The following items were paid by cash

| Petty Cash Voucher | |
|---|---|
| Date: | 05.06.XX |
| Voucher No: | 010 |
| Details | £ |
| Refreshments (no Vat) | 9.90 |
| Authorised By; | *Dennis Cope* |
| Receipt attached | |

| Petty Cash Voucher | |
|---|---|
| Date: | 10.06.XX |
| Voucher No: | 011 |
| Details | £ |
| Office stationery | 11.25 |
| VAT | 2.25 |
| Total | 13.50 |
| Authorised By; | *Dennis Cope* |
| Receipt attached | |

## TASK 8.2

Reimburse the petty cash tin with £23.40 which has been withdrawn from the bank. Use 10th June 20XX and reference TRF02 for this transaction.

## TASK 9

On the 23rd June, a member of staff purchases 'Mens Footwear' from you and pays you a total of £77.59 in cash. This is inclusive of VAT. Enter this in to the bank current account and use reference F027 for the transaction.

**TASK 10**

Produce the following reports:

(1)     Trial Balance Report

(2)     Sales Day Book

(3)     Customer Activity Report

(4)     Supplier Activity Report

(5)     Aged Creditors Report (detailed)

(6)     Aged Debtors Report (detailed)

(7)     Nominal Ledger Activity Report for the following accounts

        (a)     Bank Current Account

        (b)     Petty Cash Account

**TASK 11.1**

Refer to the following standing order schedule:

- Set up a recurring entry as shown in the standing order schedule below.
- **Produce a screen shot** of the screen setting up the recurring entry.
- Process the first payment.

| Details | Amount | Frequency of payment | Total number of payments | Payment start date 20XX | Payment finish date 20XX |
|---------|--------|----------------------|--------------------------|-------------------------|--------------------------|
| Electricity (ECBE Ltd) | £193.00 No Vat | Quarterly | 4 | 25th June 20XX | 25th March 20XX |

**TASK 11.2**

Refer to the following BACS receipt schedule:

- Set up a recurring entry as shown in the schedule below.
- **Produce a screen shot** of the screen setting up the recurring entry.
- Process the first receipt.

| Details | Amount | Frequency of receipt | Total number of receipts | Start date 20XX | Finish date 20XX |
|---------|--------|----------------------|--------------------------|-----------------|------------------|
| Rent | £1500 (no VAT) | Quarterly | 4 | 25th June 20XX | 25th March 20XX |

**TASK 12**

Enter the following journal.

<table>
<tr><td colspan="4" align="center">**JOURNAL No: 209**</td></tr>
<tr><td>**Date**</td><td>**Account Name & Code**</td><td align="center">**Dr**</td><td align="center">**Cr**</td></tr>
<tr><td>25th June</td><td>Drawings</td><td align="center">3200.00</td><td></td></tr>
<tr><td></td><td>Bank</td><td></td><td align="center">3200.00</td></tr>
<tr><td colspan="4">Being the transfer of cash for personal use.</td></tr>
</table>

**TASK 13**

On 22nd June you sold Ladies Footwear to a customer and they paid £54.00 debit card inclusive of tax £9.00. Use reference DC03.

## TASK 14

You are given the following bank statement and are asked to produce a bank reconciliation at 30th June 20XX, processing any adjustments that may be necessary. The BACS receipt on the 25th June relates to Rent Received.

**Friendly Bank plc**

201 Lake Rise
Whitewater
Cumbria
C21 9JF

STATEMENT : ACCOUNT No 22567767

**Shoes 4U**                                                   30th June 20XX
85 Barrington Close                                   Statement 0011
Carlisle
Cumbria
C41 3ED

| Date June 20XX | Detail | Paid out £ | Paid in £ | Balance |
|---|---|---|---|---|
| 1st June | Opening Balance | | | 19363.00C |
| 1st June | Transfer | 5000.00 | | 14363.00C |
| 14th June | Counter debit | 23.40 | | 14339.60C |
| 14th June | Cheque receipt | | 4811.88 | 19151.48C |
| 14th June | Cheque receipt | | 961.98 | 20113.46C |
| 18th June | Cheque 109888 | 23300.00 | | 3186.54D |
| 21st June | Debit Card transaction | | 54.00 | 3132.54D |
| 22nd June | DD – ECBE Ltd | 193.00 | | 3325.54D |
| 23rd June | Counter credit | | 77.59 | 3247.95D |
| 25th June | Counter Debit | 3200.00 | | 6447.95D |
| 25th June | Bank Charges | 50.00 | | 6497.95D |
| 25th June | BACS receipt | | 1500.00 | 4997.95D |
| 30th June | Counter Credit | | 3828.75 | 1169.20D |

| C = Credit | D = Debit | DD – Direct Debit |
|---|---|---|

**TASK 15**

Produce the following reports:

(1)    Trial Balance for the month of June (Inc. opening balances)

(2)    Detailed Audit Trail (including bank reconciled items)

(3)    Nominal Ledger Activity Report for the following accounts:

    (a)    Trade Creditors

    (b)    Sales – Ladies Footwear

(4)    Aged Debtors Analysis (detailed)

# PRACTICE PAPER 4

## SPORTS GEAR

### THE SITUATION

This assignment is based on an existing business, **Sports Gear**, who has recently set up in business selling sports equipment.

The owner of the business is Nina Birk who operates as a sole trader.

At the start of the business Nina operated a manual bookkeeping system but has now decided that from 1st July 20XX the accounting system will become computerised.

You can assume that all documentation has been checked and authorised by Nina Birk.

Some nominal ledger accounts have already been allocated suitable account codes. **You may need to amend or create other account codes.**

Sport Gear's Financial Year starts in July.

Their company details are:-

Sports Gear

34 Hockey Avenue

Tennison

London

EC1V 1NY

Tel: 01234 567891

You are employed as an accounting technician.

The business is registered for VAT. The rate of VAT charged on all goods and services sold by Sports Gear is 20%.  VAT registration number 123456789.

## TASK 1

Refer to the customer listing below and set up customer records to open Sales Ledger accounts for each customer.

| Customer account code | Customer name, address and contact details | Customer account details |
|---|---|---|
| SL01 | J Hollingham<br>56 Glencoe Avenue<br>Gants Hill<br>Ilford<br>Essex  IG1 6FR | Credit limit:           £5000<br>Payment Terms:       30 days<br>Opening Balance:     £3462.12<br>(relates to invoice 1001 dated 12th June  20XX) |
| SL02 | Paul McCallum<br>34 St Albans Road<br>Seven Kings<br>Essex  IG7 8DS | Credit limit: £9500<br>Payment Terms: 30 days<br>Opening Balance: £514.68<br>(relates to invoice 0087 dated 10th June 20XX) |
| SL03 | Kerry Jenkins<br>34 Gloucester Road<br>Gillingham<br>Kent   ME14 3TL | Credit limit:           £8000<br>Payment Terms:       30 days<br>Opening Balance:     £758.34<br>(relates to invoice 0093 dated 8th June 20XX) |
| SL04 | Harry Bucket<br>54 Dale Road<br>Harrogate<br>North Yorks  Y02 3HN | Credit limit:           £12000<br>Payment Terms:       30 days<br>Opening Balance:     £2767.34<br>(relates to invoice 1003 dated 12th June 20XX) |
| SL05 | Evelyn Rose<br>98 Crabtree Drive<br>Bromley<br>Kent  DA3 6AY | Credit limit:           £7000<br>Payment Terms:       30 days<br>Opening Balance:     £942.98<br>(relates to invoice 1004 dated 12th June 20XX) |

## TASK 2

Refer to the supplier listing below and set up supplier records to open Purchase Ledger account for each supplier.

| Supplier account code | Supplier name, address and contact details | Supplier account details |
|---|---|---|
| PL01 | Radcliff and Sons<br>Orient House<br>Lower Clapham<br>London  E1 2RH | Credit limit:          £15500<br>Payment Terms:     30 days<br>Opening Balance:  £5362.14<br>(relates to invoice 1874 dated 22nd June 20XX) |
| PL02 | Tennison Bros<br>White Cottage<br>London  WC1 6YD | Credit limit:          £11000<br>Payment Terms:     30 days<br>Opening Balance:  £2801.00<br>(relates to invoice B-321 dated 11th June 20XX) |
| PL03 | Skipton & Co<br>22 Chatsworth Lane<br>Water Square<br>London  EC1V 6NJ | Credit limit:          £9000<br>Payment Terms:     30 days<br>Opening Balance:  £501.00<br>(relates to invoice 1087 dated 11th June 20XX) |
| PL04 | Evelyn Rose<br>98 Crabtree Drive<br>Bromley<br>Kent  DA3 6AY | Credit limit:          £3000<br>Payment Terms:     30 days<br>Opening Balance:  £250.00<br>(relates to invoice A193 dated 18th June 20XX) |

## TASK 3.1

Refer to the list of General ledger balances below. Enter the opening balances into the computer, making sure you select/create/amend any ledger accounts where necessary.

List of general ledger balances as at 01.07.20XX

| Account name | £ | £ |
|---|---|---|
| Motor Vehicle | 15500.00 | |
| Furniture and Fixtures | 18000.00 | |
| Office Equipment | 8430.00 | |
| Bank | 3325.40 | |
| Petty Cash | 300.00 | |
| Sales Ledger Control Account* | 8445.46 | |
| Purchase Ledger Control Account* | | 8914.14 |
| VAT on Sales | | 3458.00 |
| VAT on Purchases | 1120.00 | |
| Capital | | 52000.00 |
| Drawings | 1294.00 | |
| Sales – Tennis Racquets | | 13266.78 |
| Sales – Exercise Bikes | | 22310.00 |
| Sales – Golf Clubs | | 9543.00 |
| Sales – Fishing Rods | | 5644.00 |
| Purchases – Tennis Racquets | 21354.00 | |
| Purchases – Exercise Bikes | 25610.00 | |
| Purchases – Golf Clubs | 5475.00 | |
| Purchases – Fishing Rods | 4796.00 | |
| Office Stationery | 430.00 | |
| Postage | 560.00 | |
| Electricity | 496.06 | |
| *Note* You do not need to enter these figures as you have already entered opening balances for customers and suppliers | | |

## TASK 3.2

Produce the following reports and **identify and correct any errors:**

- Customer Address list
- Supplier Address List
- Period Trial Balance Report

## TASK 4

Enter the following sales invoices and credit notes onto the computer.

---

**INVOICE**

Sports Gear

34 Hockey Avenue

Tennison

London

EC1V 1NY

| | |
|---|---|
| Account No: SL01 | Date: 4 July 20XX |
| Invoice No: 1052 | |

J Hollingham

56 Glencoe Avenue

Gants Hill

Ilford

Essex

IG1 6FR

| Quantity | Description | Unit Price | Net £ | Tax £ | Gross £ | Nominal code |
|---|---|---|---|---|---|---|
| 20 | Tennis Racquets | 44.10 | 882.00 | 176.40 | 1058.40 | 4000 |
| 10 | Exercise Bikes | 102.36 | 1023.60 | 204.72 | 1228.32 | 4001 |
| 6 | Fishing Rods | 54.00 | 324.00 | 64.80 | 388.80 | 4003 |

Terms 30 days

---

**INVOICE**

Sports Gear

34 Hockey Avenue

Tennison

London

EC1V 1NY

| | |
|---|---|
| Account No: SL03 | Date: 6 July 20XX |
| Invoice No: 1053 | |

Kerry Jenkins

Gloucester Road

Gillingham

Kent

ME14 3TL

| Quantity | Description | Unit Price | Net £ | Tax £ | Gross £ | Nominal code |
|---|---|---|---|---|---|---|
| 3 | Tennis Racquets | 44.10 | 132.30 | 26.46 | 158.76 | 4000 |

Terms 30 days

---

**INVOICE**

Sports Gear

34 Hockey Avenue

Tennison

London

EC1V 1NY

Account No:    SL04                    Date: 8 July 20XX

Invoice No:    1054

Harry Bucket

54 Dale Road

Yorkshire

Y02 3HN

| Quantity | Description | Unit Price | Net £ | Tax £ | Gross £ | Nominal code |
|---|---|---|---|---|---|---|
| 18 | Golf Clubs | 84.10 | 1513.80 | 302.76 | 1816.56 | 4002 |

Terms 30 days

**CREDIT NOTE**

Sports Gear

34 Hockey Avenue

Tennison

London

EC1V 1NY

Account No:    SL01                    Date: 17 July 20XX

Invoice No:    CR34

J Hollingham

56 Glencoe Avenue

Gants Hill

Ilford

Essex

IG1 6FR

| **Description** | £ |
|---|---|
| Return faulty Exercise Bike | 510.63 |
| | |
| VAT @ 20.0% | 102.12 |
| Total credit | 612.75 |

## TASK 5

Enter the purchases invoices into the computer. Check the nominal codes before entering the invoices and create/amend any ledger accounts where necessary.

| Date | A/C No. | Invoice Ref | Description | Net | Vat | Gross | Nominal code |
|------|---------|-------------|-------------|-----|-----|-------|--------------|
| 3 July | PL01 | 1099 | Tennis Racquets | 550.00 | 110.00 | 660.00 | 5000 |
| 5 July | PL02 | B – 1147 | Exercise Bikes | 320.00 | 64.00 | 384.00 | 5001 |
| 5 July | PL02 | B – 1147 | Postage | 35.00 | 0.00 | 35.00 | 7510 |
| 10 July | PL03 | 2785 | Golf Clubs | 938.00 | 187.60 | 1125.60 | 5002 |
| 10 July | PL04 | A/5698 | Fishing Rods | 671.00 | 134.20 | 805.20 | 5003 |

## TASK 6

On 19th July, you receive a credit note (CX432) from Skipton & Co (Account No PL03) for two Golf Clubs that had been returned to them. The total credit note is for 109.45 plus sales tax of 20%.

## TASK 7

The following payments were received from customers; enter the receipts on the accounts system.

| Date | Receipt type | Customer | Amount | Details |
|------|--------------|----------|--------|---------|
| 19 July | Cheque No. 542321 | J Hollingham | 2849.37 | Payment for invoice 1001 including credit note CR34 |
| 12 July | Cheque No. 222547 | Kerry Jenkins | 758.34 | Payment for invoice 0093 |
| 13 July | BACS | Harry Bucket | 2767.34 | Payment for invoice 1003 |

## TASK 8

The following cheque payments were sent to suppliers; enter the payments on the accounts system and **raise the relevant remittance advices.**

| Date | Cheque No: | Supplier | Amount | Details |
|------|-----------|----------|--------|---------|
| 14th July | 170012 | Radcliff & Sons | 5362.14 | Payment for invoice 1874 |
| 17th July | 170013 | Tennison Bros | 2801.00 | Payment for invoice B-321 |

## TASK 9

Enter the Petty cash payments into the computer

| Petty Cash Voucher | |
|---|---|
| **Date:** | 10.07.XX |
| **Voucher No:** | 152 |
| **Details** | £ |
| Stationery (no Vat) | 19.90 |
| **Authorised By;** | *Nina Birk* |
| Receipt attached | |

| Petty Cash Voucher | |
|---|---|
| **Date:** | 20.07.XX |
| **Voucher No:** | 187 |
| **Details** | £ |
| Postage | 343.55 |
| VAT | 68.71 |
| Total | 412.26 |
| **Authorised By;** | *Nina Birk* |
| Receipt attached | |

## TASK 10

Refer to the following cash sales and enter receipts into the bank current account on the computer.

| Date | Receipt ref | Gross | VAT | NET | Nominal code |
|---|---|---|---|---|---|
| 13 July | REC101 | 1,200.00 | 200.00 | 1,000.00 | 4000 |
| 15 July | REC102 | 2,879.40 | 479.90 | 2,399.50 | 4001 |
| 15 July | REC103 | 1,194.90 | 199.15 | 995.75 | 4000 |

## TASK 11

Produce the following reports:

- Trial Balance Report
- Sales Day Book
- Purchase Day Book
- Customer Activity Report
- Supplier Activity Report
- Aged Creditors Report
- Aged Debtors Report
- Produce a Statement for Paul McCallum

## TASK 12

Enter the following journal

<table>
<tr><th colspan="4">Ref : JNL004</th></tr>
<tr><th>Date</th><th>Account Name & Code</th><th>Dr</th><th>Cr</th></tr>
<tr><td>25.07.XX</td><td>Drawings</td><td>3,441.00</td><td></td></tr>
<tr><td></td><td>Bank</td><td></td><td>3,441.00</td></tr>
<tr><td colspan="4">Being the transfer of cash for personal use.</td></tr>
</table>

## TASK 13

Refer to the following email below from Nina Birk and **save a screenshot of your work** and save with a **suitable file name**.

| E-Mail | |
|---|---|
| From: | Nina Birk |
| Date: | 19th July 20XX |
| Subject: | Customer change of address |

Hello

A credit customer Harry Bucket has moved premises. New address as follows:

137 Chester Road

Capel Corner

CR3 2SA

Telephone: 08459 754 256

Please ensure that this is updated on the computerised accounts system.

Thanks

Nina

## TASK 14

The following cheque payments were sent to suppliers; enter the payments on the accounts system.

| Date | A/c No | Supplier | Cheque No | Details | Amount |
|---|---|---|---|---|---|
| 28 July | PL03 | Skipton & Co | 170014 | Invoice 1087 | 501.00 |
| 28 July | PL01 | Radcliff & Sons | 170015 | Invoice 1099 | 660.00 |

## TASK 15

The following payments were received from customers; enter the receipts on the accounts system.

| Date | Customer | Cheque No | Details | Amount (£) |
|---|---|---|---|---|
| 28 July | J Hollingham | 087651 | Invoice 1052 | 2675.52 |
| 28 July | Harry Bucket | 198871 | Invoice 1054 | Part Payment of 500.00 |

## TASK 16

On 14th July a member of staff buys a Tennis Racquet paying you £50.00 in Cash. This is inclusive of sales tax. Enter this in to the bank current account and use reference ST5 for the transaction.

## TASK 17

On 19th July, you sold a 'Golf Club' to a customer and they paid £45.00 (Plus VAT) debit card. Use reference CS03.

## TASK 18

You are asked to set up a monthly standing order for Insurance for £100.00 (Exempt VAT) for a period of 12 months commencing on 28th July. There is no VAT on this transaction. The Insurance is payable to Ipswich Union. Choose a suitable nominal code for Insurance. **Take a screenshot** of the details and save as a 'Word' document with a suitable file name. Process July's payment.

**TASK 19**

You are given the following bank statement and are asked to produce a bank reconciliation at 31st July, processing any adjustments that may be necessary.

**Sully Bank plc**

201 Main Road

Gillingham

Kent

ME3 5TF

Sports Gear
34 Hockey Avenue
Tennison
London
EC1V 1NY

31st July 20XX
Statement no: 1001

Account number 00678432

**Statement of Account**

| Date: July 2011 | Details | Paid out £ | Paid in £ | Balance £ |
|---|---|---|---|---|
| 01 July | Opening balance | | | 3325.40C |
| 12 July | Counter Credit | | 758.34 | 4083.74C |
| 13 July | BACS | | 2767.34 | 6851.08C |
| 13 July | Counter credit | | 1200.00 | 8051.08C |
| 14 July | Counter credit | | 50.00 | 8101.08C |
| 15 July | Counter credit | | 2879.40 | 10980.48C |
| 15 July | Counter credit | | 1194.90 | 12175.38C |
| 19 July | Cheque 170013 | 2801.00 | | 9374.38C |
| 20 July | Counter Credit | | 2849.37 | 12223.75C |
| 20 July | Debit Card | | 54.00 | 12277.75C |
| 25 July | Counter Debit | 3441.00 | | 8836.75C |
| 29 July | Counter Credit | | 2675.52 | 11512.27C |
| 29 July | Counter Credit | | 500.00 | 12012.27C |
| 29 July | Standing Order – Ipswich Union | 100.00 | | 11912.27C |
| 31 July | Bank charges | 32.19 | | 11880.08C |
| | D = Debit C = Credit | | | |

**TASK 20**

Transfer £432.16 from the bank current account to the petty cash account. Use reference TRF01 for this transaction and date it 31st July.

## TASK 21

Produce the following reports

- Customer Address List
- Customer Activity (detailed report)
- Supplier Activity (detailed report)
- Period Trial Balance for the month of July (inc. opening balances)
- Nominal Ledger Activity Report for the following accounts
    - Bank Current Account
    - Petty Cash Account

# PRACTICE PAPER 5

## WAY TO WORK

### THE SITUATION

This assignment is based on an existing business, Way to Work.

At the start of the business they operated under a manual bookkeeping system but they have now decided that from 1st March 20XX the accounting system will become computerised.

Some nominal ledger accounts have already been allocated suitable account codes. **You may need to amend or create other account codes.**

Way to Work's financial year starts in March.

Their company details are:-

Way to Work

55 Upper Street

London

N1 9PE

Tel: 01234 567891

You are employed as an accounting technician.

The business is registered for VAT. The company's products are standard rated for VAT (20%). VAT registration number 123456789.

Set the company's financial year to start in March 20XX

**TASK 1**

Refer to the customer listing below and set up customer records to open Sales Ledger accounts for each customer.

| Customer account code | Customer name, address and contact details | Customer account details |
|---|---|---|
| JP01 | Morgan, Smith & Winston<br>City Road<br>Islington<br>London<br>N1 9PL | Credit limit: £7000<br>Payment Terms: 30 days<br>Opening Balance: £1172.34<br>(relates to invoice INV021 dated 14th February 20XX) |
| JP02 | Cyril West<br>Grays West<br>Grays Inn Road<br>London<br>WC1 1LT | Credit limit: £8500<br>Payment Terms: 30 days<br>Opening Balance: £2954.00<br>(relates to invoice INV045 dated 22nd February 20XX). |
| JP03 | Wallace & Gromit Ltd<br>134 Upper Street<br>Islington<br>London<br>N1 2PT | Credit limit: £17000<br>Payment Terms: 30 days<br>Opening Balance: £3180.00<br>(relates to invoice INV033 dated 18th February 20XX) |
| JP04 | Star Paper<br>66 White Lion Street<br>London<br>N1 5RX | Credit limit: £12500<br>Payment Terms: 30 days<br>Opening Balance: £1867.34<br>(relates to invoice INV034 dated 22nd February 20XX) |

## TASK 2

Refer to the supplier listing below and set up supplier records to open Purchase Ledger accounts for each supplier.

| Supplier account code | Supplier name, address and contact details | Supplier account details |
|---|---|---|
| SP01 | Paper Products UK<br>South Down Trading Estate<br>Sheffield<br>S15 4DR | Credit limit: £8500<br>Payment Terms: 30 days<br>Opening Balance: £445.23<br>(relates to invoice 0165 dated 28th February 20XX). |
| SP02 | Wallace & Gromit Ltd<br>134 Upper Street<br>Islington<br>London<br>N1 2PT | Credit limit: £12000<br>Payment Terms: 30 days<br>Opening Balance: £6711.00<br>(relates to invoice 02183 dated 11th February 20XX) |
| SP03 | Whole Office Furniture<br>176 East Way<br>Leeds<br>LD4 6PP | Credit limit: £4000<br>Payment Terms: 30 days<br>Opening Balance: £1875.21<br>(relates to invoice 1028 dated 26th February 20XX) |
| SP04 | Stationery World<br>32 Great Portland Road<br>London<br>WC1V 6HH | Credit limit: £16500<br>Payment Terms: 30 days<br>Opening Balance: £9504.32<br>(relates to invoice 0187 dated 18th February 20XX). |

## TASK 3.1

Refer to the list of General ledger balances below. Enter the opening balances into the computer, making sure you select/create/amend the appropriate general ledger account codes.

List of general ledger balances as at 01.03.20XX

| Account name | £ | £ |
|---|---|---|
| Motor Vehicle | 14000.00 | |
| Furniture and Fixtures | 8000.00 | |
| Bank | 6210.81 | |
| Petty Cash | 100.00 | |
| Sales Ledger Control Account * | 9173.68 | |
| Purchase Ledger Control Account* | | 18535.76 |
| Capital | | 34000.00 |
| Drawings | 1000.00 | |
| Stationery Sales | | 903.73 |
| CD Roms Sales | | 855.00 |
| Printer Accessories Sales | | 9842.00 |
| Stationery purchases | 2400.00 | |
| CD Rom purchases | 210.00 | |
| Printer Accessory purchases | 15000.00 | |
| Wages and Salaries | 5600.00 | |
| General Expenses | 342.00 | |
| Rent | 2100.00 | |
| *Note* <br><br> You do not need to enter these figures as you have already entered opening balances for customers and suppliers. | | |

## TASK 3.2

Transfer £1500.00 from the bank current account to the bank deposit account. Date the transaction 1st March and use reference TRANS01.

## TASK 3.3

Produce the following reports and **identify and correct any errors**.

- Customer Address List
- Supplier Address List
- Trial Balance

**TASK 4**

Enter the sales invoices onto the computer.

| Date | A/C No. | Invoice Ref | Description | Nominal Code | Gross £ | VAT £ | Net £ |
|------|---------|-------------|-------------|--------------|---------|-------|-------|
| 3 Mar | JP02 | INV041 | Stationery | 4000 | 936.00 | 156.00 | 780.00 |
| 3 Mar | JP04 | INV042 | CD Roms | 4001 | 1105.20 | 184.20 | 921.00 |
| 5 Mar | JP01 | INV043 | Printer Accessory | 4002 | 5251.20 | 875.20 | 4376.00 |
| 7 Mar | JP03 | INV044 | Printer Accessory | 4002 | 549.60 | 91.60 | 458.00 |
| 7 Mar | JP01 | INV045 | Stationery | 4000 | 7452.00 | 1242.00 | 6210.00 |

**TASK 5**

On 17th March you send a credit note (CR51) to Star Paper (Account No JP04) for Printer Accessories.

The total is £251.27 plus tax.

**TASK 6**

Enter the purchases invoices into the computer.

| Date | A/C No. | Invoice Ref | Description | Nominal Code | Gross | Vat | Net |
|------|---------|-------------|-------------|--------------|-------|-----|-----|
| 10 Mar | SP01 | 0200 | Stationery | 5000 | 586.80 | 97.80 | 489.00 |
| 11 Mar | SP02 | 02241 | CD Roms | 5001 | 414.00 | 69.00 | 345.00 |
| 11 Mar | SP03 | 1098 | Printer Accessory | 5002 | 9153.60 | 1525.60 | 7628.00 |
| 14 Mar | SP04 | 0197 | Stationery | 5000 | 4280.40 | 713.40 | 3567.00 |

**TASK 7**

Enter the following purchase credit note onto the computer system.

| Date | A/C No | Supplier | N/C | Credit Note Ref | Amount | Details |
|------|--------|----------|-----|-----------------|--------|---------|
| 19 Mar | SP04 | Stationery World | 5000 | RF287 | 124.08 | Plus Tax |

**TASK 8**

The following payments were received from customers; enter the receipts on the accounts system.

| Date | Cheque Number | Customer | Amount | Details |
|------|---------------|----------|--------|---------|
| 15 Mar | 203998 | Morgan, Smith & Winston | 1172.34 | Payment for invoice INV021 |
| 17 Mar | 103112 | Cyril West | 2954.00 | Payment for invoice INV045 |
| 19 Mar | 011211 | Star Paper | 1565.82 | Payment for invoice INV034 including credit note CR51 |

## TASK 9

The following cheque payments were sent to suppliers; enter the payments on the accounts system dated 31st March, and **raise the relevant remittance advices**.

| Supplier | Cheque No: | Amount | Details |
|---|---|---|---|
| Paper Products UK | 100076 | 445.23 | Payment for invoice 0165 |
| Whole Office Furniture | 100077 | 1875.21 | Payment for invoice 1028 |
| Stationery World | 100078 | 9504.32 | Payment for invoice 0187 |

## TASK 10

On 15th March you transfer £600.00 from the Bank account to the Petty Cash account. Use reference TRANS02 for this transaction.

## TASK 11

Enter the following petty cash payments into the computer. Check the nominal codes before entering the payments and select/create/amend any ledger accounts where necessary.

| Date | Ref | Nominal Code | Details | Net | VAT | Gross |
|---|---|---|---|---|---|---|
| 19 Mar | 056 | 7200 | Electricity | 84.10 | 16.82 | 100.92 |
| 20 Mar | 057 | 6201 | Advertising | 327.00 | 65.40 | 392.40 |

## TASK 12

On the 28th March, a member of staff purchases a 'Printer Accessories' from you and pays you a total of £123.48 in cash. This is inclusive of VAT of £20.58. Use reference ST4 for this transaction and enter the funds in to the bank current account.

## TASK 13

On the 31st March you are asked to set up a monthly standing order for Rent for £568.00 (Exempt VAT) for a period of 12 months commencing on 31st March. The Rent is payable to ICPW Bank. Process the payment for March.

**TASK 14**

You are given the following bank statement and are asked to produce a bank reconciliation at 31st March, processing any adjustments that may be necessary.

**Islington Bank Plc**

201 Upper Street

Islington

London

N1 9PE

Way to Work
55 Upper Street
London
N1 9PE

31st March 20XX

Statement no: 0002

Account number: 32543211

**Statement of Account**

| Date: March 20XX | Details | Paid out £ | Paid in £ | Balance £ |
|---|---|---|---|---|
| 01 Mar | Opening balance | | | 6210.81C |
| 01 Mar | Transfer | 1500.00 | | 4710.81C |
| 15 Mar | Transfer | 600.00 | | 4110.81C |
| 18 Mar | Counter Credit | | 1172.34 | 5283.15C |
| 18 Mar | Counter Credit | | 2954.00 | 8237.15C |
| 19 Mar | Counter Credit | | 1565.82 | 9802.97C |
| 26 Mar | 100017 | 1875.21 | | 7927.76C |
| 28 Mar | Counter credit | | 123.48 | 8051.24C |
| 31 Mar | 100076 | 445.23 | | 7606.01C |
| 31 Mar | Standing Order – ICPW Bank | 568.00 | | 7038.01C |
| 31 Mar | Bank Charges | 123.45 | | 6914.56C |
| | D = Debit C = Credit | | | |

**TASK 15**

Produce the following reports

- Customer Activity (detailed report)
- Supplier Activity (detailed report)
- Trial Balance for the month of March (including opening balances)
- Audit Trial for March only (inc opening balances)
- Nominal Ledger Activity Report for the following accounts
    - Bank Current Account
    - Petty Cash Account

# Section 2

# ANSWERS TO PRACTICE QUESTIONS

## PRACTICE PAPER 1

### TOY SHOP ANSWERS

### TASK 3.3

### Customer Address List

| | Toy Shop | | | | 20 Apr 2017 |
| --- | --- | --- | --- | --- | --- |
| | Customer Address List | | | | 13:51 |

Address Types: All

| Customer Name | Address | Contact name | Phone | Mobile | Email | Fax |
| --- | --- | --- | --- | --- | --- | --- |
| Busy Bee Toys (BB01) | 832 High Street<br>Oxford<br>OX2 3WG | Main Contact | | | | |
| Forming Fun (FF02) | 21 Newton Quay<br>Knott Mill<br>Manchester<br>M6 3RJ | Main Contact | | | | |
| Space Models (SM03) | 13 Central Street<br>Perth<br>Scotland<br>SC4 8RQ | Main Contact | | | | |
| Teddy T's Party (TP04) | 3 Paradise Street<br>Wokingham<br>WO4 6QP | Main Contact | | | | |

## TASK 3.3

### Supplier Address List

Address Types: All

| Supplier Name | Address | Contact name | Phone | Mobile | Email | Fax |
|---|---|---|---|---|---|---|
| Abacus C & C (PL01) | Unit 31<br>Kitts Industrial Estate<br>St Helens<br>Lancs | Main Contact | | | | |
| Compugames Ltd (PL02) | 6 Jury Road<br>Dublin<br>Eire | Main Contact | | | | |
| Space Models (PL03) | 13 Central Street<br>Perth<br>Scotland | Main Contact | | | | |
| Toys Unlimited (PL04) | 95 Cuscaden Road<br>Edinburgh<br>Scotland | Main Contact | | | | |

## TASK 3.3

### Period Trial Balance Report

From: 30/04/2016
To:   30/04/2017

Toy Shop
**Trial Balance Report**

20 Apr 2017
13:57

This period only

| Nominal Code | Name | Debit | Credit |
|---|---|---|---|
| | | **Selected Period** | |
| 0040 | Fixtures and fittings - Cost | 5,800.00 | |
| 0050 | Motor Vehicles - Cost | 3,000.00 | |
| 1100 | Trade Debtors | 2,223.60 | |
| 1200 | Current | 3,725.00 | |
| 1210 | Cash | 300.00 | |
| 1220 | Deposit | 500.00 | |
| 2100 | Trade Creditors | | 2,157.60 |
| 2200 | VAT on Sales | | 543.00 |
| 2201 | VAT on Purchases | 109.00 | |
| 3200 | Capital introduced | | 20,000.00 |
| 3260 | Drawings - equity | 355.00 | |
| 4000 | Sales - Computer Games | | 6,080.00 |
| 4001 | Sales - Jigsaws | | 700.00 |
| 4002 | Sales - Boxed Games | | 1,967.00 |
| 5000 | Purchases - Computer Games | 8,000.00 | |
| 5001 | Purchases - Jigsaws | 3,200.00 | |
| 5002 | Purchases - Boxed Games | 2,465.00 | |
| 7100 | Rent and rates | 1,550.00 | |
| 7200 | Electricity | 167.00 | |
| 7500 | Office Stationery | 53.00 | |
| | TOTAL | £31,447.60 | £31,447.60 |

## TASK 7

### Abacus C & C – remittance advice

# Remittance Advice

Date Paid: 22/05/2016

Reference: PL01

| **Abacus C & C**<br>Unit 31<br>Kitts Industrial Estate<br>St Helens<br>Lancs | **Toy Shop**<br>64 Long Lane<br>Langhorne<br>North Yorkshire<br>YO21 3EJ<br>United Kingdom<br><br>Telephone: 01234 567891<br><br>VAT Number: GB 123456789 |
|---|---|

**Reference:** Chq no 101333

| Our Ref | Your Ref | Date | Total Amount | Amount Paid |
|---|---|---|---|---|
| Inv B/1874 | | 30/04/2016 | 369.60 | 369.60 |
| | | **Total Paid:** | | **£ 369.60 GBP** |

### Compugames – remittance advice

# Remittance Advice

Date Paid: 22/05/2016

Reference: PL02

| **Compugames Ltd**<br>6 Jury Road<br>Dublin<br>Eire | **Toy Shop**<br>64 Long Lane<br>Langhorne<br>North Yorkshire<br>YO21 3EJ<br>United Kingdom<br><br>Telephone: 01234 567891<br><br>VAT Number: GB 123456789 |
|---|---|

**Reference:** Chq no 101334

| Our Ref | Your Ref | Date | Total Amount | Amount Paid |
|---|---|---|---|---|
| Inv 1087 | | 30/04/2016 | 511.20 | 511.20 |
| 145215 | | 05/05/2016 | 600.00 | 600.00 |
| CR 11245 | | 15/05/2016 | -105.60 | -105.60 |
| | | **Total Paid:** | | **£ 1,005.60 GBP** |

## TASK 11

### Trial Balance Report

Toy Shop
**Trial Balance Report**

This period only

| Nominal Code | Name | Selected Period | |
|---|---|---|---|
| | | Debit | Credit |
| 0040 | Fixtures and fittings - Cost | 5,800.00 | |
| 0050 | Motor Vehicles - Cost | 3,000.00 | |
| 1100 | Trade Debtors | 10,897.20 | |
| 1200 | Current | 6,068.60 | |
| 1210 | Cash | 255.52 | |
| 1220 | Deposit | 500.00 | |
| 2100 | Trade Creditors | | 3,034.80 |
| 2200 | VAT on Sales | | 2,775.90 |
| 2201 | VAT on Purchases | 483.48 | |
| 3200 | Capital introduced | | 20,000.00 |
| 3260 | Drawings - equity | 2,355.00 | |
| 4000 | Sales - Computer Games | | 15,340.00 |
| 4001 | Sales - Jigsaws | | 3,099.50 |
| 4002 | Sales - Boxed Games | | 2,467.00 |
| 5000 | Purchases - Computer Games | 9,362.00 | |
| 5001 | Purchases - Jigsaws | 3,218.00 | |
| 5002 | Purchases - Boxed Games | 2,965.00 | |
| 7100 | Rent and rates | 1,550.00 | |
| 7200 | Electricity | 167.00 | |
| 7500 | Office Stationery | 53.00 | |
| 8201 | Subscriptions | 32.00 | |
| 8205 | Refreshments | 10.40 | |
| | **TOTAL** | **£46,717.20** | **£46,717.20** |

## TASK 11

### Sales Day Book

From: 30/04/2016
To: 31/05/2016

Toy Shop
**Sales Day Book Report**

20 Apr 2017
15:33

Type: Sales QE Invoice

| Trx No | Type | Date | Name | Invoice Number | Ref | Details | Net | VAT | Total |
|--------|------|------|------|----------------|-----|---------|-----|-----|-------|
| 14 | Sales QE Invoice | 04/05/2016 | Busy Bee Toys | | Inv 2021 | | 2,585.00 | 517.00 | 3,102.00 |
| 15 | Sales QE Invoice | 04/05/2016 | Forming Fun | | Inv 2022 | | 500.00 | 100.00 | 600.00 |
| 16 | Sales QE Invoice | 06/05/2016 | Teddy T's Party | | Inv 2023 | | 5,000.00 | 1,000.00 | 6,000.00 |
| | | | | | | TOTAL | £8,085.00 | £1,617.00 | £9,702.00 |

## TASK 11

### Sales Return Day Book

From: 30/04/2016
To: 31/05/2016

Toy Shop
**Sales Day Book Report**

20 Apr 2017
15:34

Type: Sales QE Credit

| Trx No | Type | Date | Name | Invoice Number | Ref | Details | Net | VAT | Total |
|--------|------|------|------|----------------|-----|---------|-----|-----|-------|
| 17 | Sales QE Credit | 13/05/2016 | Teddy T's Party | | CN101 | Return faulty computer games | -320.00 | -64.00 | -384.00 |
| | | | | | | TOTAL | -£320.00 | -£64.00 | -£384.00 |

## TASK 11

### Purchase Day Book

From: 30/04/2016
To: 31/05/2016

Toy Shop
**Purchase Day Book Report**

20 Apr 2017
15:36

Type: Purchase QE Invoice

| Trx No | Type | Date | Name | Invoice Number | Ref | Details | Net | VAT | Total |
|--------|------|------|------|----------------|-----|---------|-----|-----|-------|
| 18 | Purchase QE Invoice | 03/05/2016 | Abacus C & C | | B/909 | | 450.00 | 90.00 | 540.00 |
| 19 | Purchase QE Invoice | 05/05/2016 | Compugames Ltd | | 145215 | | 500.00 | 100.00 | 600.00 |
| 20 | Purchase QE Invoice | 10/05/2016 | Space Models | | C-32632 | | 1,000.00 | 200.00 | 1,200.00 |
| 34 | Purchase QE Invoice | 10/05/2016 | Toys Unlimited | | 12421 | | 18.00 | 0.00 | 18.00 |
| | | | | | | TOTAL | £1,968.00 | £390.00 | £2,358.00 |

## TASK 11

### Customer Activity Report

**Busy Bee Toys (BB01)**

| Date | Number | Reference | Type | Net | VAT | Total | Discount | Outstanding |
|---|---|---|---|---|---|---|---|---|
| 30/04/2016 | | Inv 021 | Customer OB Invoice | 349.20 | 0.00 | 349.20 | | 0.00 |
| 04/05/2016 | | Inv 2021 | Sales QE Invoice | 2,585.00 | 517.00 | 3,102.00 | | 3,102.00 |
| 17/05/2016 | | Chq no 100322 | Customer Receipt | | | -349.20 | 0.00 | 0.00 |
| | | | | | | 3,102.00 | | 3,102.00 |

**Forming Fun (FF02)**

| Date | Number | Reference | Type | Net | VAT | Total | Discount | Outstanding |
|---|---|---|---|---|---|---|---|---|
| 30/04/2016 | | Inv 035 | Customer OB Invoice | 99.60 | 0.00 | 99.60 | | 0.00 |
| 04/05/2016 | | Inv 2022 | Sales QE Invoice | 500.00 | 100.00 | 600.00 | | 600.00 |
| 17/05/2016 | | Chq no 267543 | Customer Receipt | | | -99.60 | 0.00 | 0.00 |
| | | | | | | 600.00 | | 600.00 |

**Space Models (SM03)**

| Date | Number | Reference | Type | Net | VAT | Total | Discount | Outstanding |
|---|---|---|---|---|---|---|---|---|
| 30/04/2016 | | Inv 093 | Customer OB Invoice | 1,195.20 | 0.00 | 1,195.20 | | 1,195.20 |
| | | | | | | 1,195.20 | | 1,195.20 |

**Teddy T's Party (TP04)**

| Date | Number | Reference | Type | Net | VAT | Total | Discount | Outstanding |
|---|---|---|---|---|---|---|---|---|
| 30/04/2016 | | Inv 1003 | Customer OB Invoice | 579.60 | 0.00 | 579.60 | | 0.00 |
| 06/05/2016 | | Inv 2023 | Sales QE Invoice | 5,000.00 | 1,000.00 | 6,000.00 | | 6,000.00 |
| 13/05/2016 | | CN101 | Sales QE Credit | -320.00 | -64.00 | -384.00 | | 0.00 |
| 26/05/2016 | | BACS | Customer Receipt | | | -195.60 | 0.00 | 0.00 |
| | | | | | | 6,000.00 | | 6,000.00 |

## TASK 11

### Supplier Activity Report

From: 30/04/2016
To:    31/05/2016

Toy Shop
**Supplier Activity Report**

20 Apr 2017
15:39

#### Abacus C & C (PL01)

| Date | Number | Reference | Type | Net | VAT | Total | Discount | Outstanding |
|---|---|---|---|---|---|---|---|---|
| 30/04/2016 | | Inv B/1874 | Supplier OB Invoice | 369.60 | 0.00 | 369.60 | | 0.00 |
| 03/05/2016 | | B/989 | Purchase QE Invoice | 450.00 | 90.00 | 540.00 | | 540.00 |
| 22/05/2016 | | Chq no 101333 | Supplier Payment | | | -369.60 | 0.00 | 0.00 |
| | | | | | | 540.00 | | 540.00 |

#### Compugames Ltd (PL02)

| Date | Number | Reference | Type | Net | VAT | Total | Discount | Outstanding |
|---|---|---|---|---|---|---|---|---|
| 30/04/2016 | | Inv 1087 | Supplier OB Invoice | 511.20 | 0.00 | 511.20 | | 0.00 |
| 05/05/2016 | | 145215 | Purchase QE Invoice | 500.00 | 100.00 | 600.00 | | 0.00 |
| 15/05/2016 | | CR 11245 | Purchase QE Credit | -88.00 | -17.60 | -105.60 | | 0.00 |
| 22/05/2016 | | Chq no 101334 | Supplier Payment | | | -1,005.60 | 0.00 | 0.00 |
| | | | | | | 0.00 | | 0.00 |

#### Space Models (PL03)

| Date | Number | Reference | Type | Net | VAT | Total | Discount | Outstanding |
|---|---|---|---|---|---|---|---|---|
| 30/04/2016 | | Inv F-0193 | Supplier OB Invoice | 306.00 | 0.00 | 306.00 | | 306.00 |
| 10/05/2016 | | C-32632 | Purchase QE Invoice | 1,000.00 | 200.00 | 1,200.00 | | 1,200.00 |
| | | | | | | 1,506.00 | | 1,506.00 |

#### Toys Unlimited (PL04)

| Date | Number | Reference | Type | Net | VAT | Total | Discount | Outstanding |
|---|---|---|---|---|---|---|---|---|
| 30/04/2016 | | Inv W/032 | Supplier OB Invoice | 970.80 | 0.00 | 970.80 | | 970.80 |
| 10/05/2016 | | 12421 | Purchase QE Invoice | 18.00 | 0.00 | 18.00 | | 18.00 |
| | | | | | | 988.80 | | 988.80 |

## TASK 11

### Aged Creditors Report

To: 31/05/2016

Toy Shop
**Aged Creditors Breakdown**

| Date | Reference | Total | Due Date | O/S Amt | < 30 days | < 60 days | < 90 days | Older |
|---|---|---|---|---|---|---|---|---|
| **Abacus C & C (PL01), Credit limit: £5,500.00** | | | | | | | | |
| **, Terms: 30 days - OVERDUE** | | | | | | | | |
| 03/05/2016 | B/989 | 540.00 | 02/06/2016 | 540.00 | 540.00 | | | |
| | | | | £540.00 | £540.00 | £0.00 | £0.00 | £0.00 |
| | | | | | | | | |
| **Space Models (PL03), Credit limit: £2,000.00** | | | | | | | | |
| **, Terms: 30 days - OVERDUE** | | | | | | | | |
| 10/05/2016 | C-32632 | 1,200.00 | 09/06/2016 | 1,200.00 | 1,200.00 | | | |
| 30/04/2016 | Inv F-0193 | 306.00 | 30/05/2016 | 306.00 | | 306.00 | | |
| | | | | £1,506.00 | £1,200.00 | £306.00 | £0.00 | £0.00 |
| | | | | | | | | |
| **Toys Unlimited (PL04), Credit limit: £2,000.00** | | | | | | | | |
| **, Terms: 30 days - OVERDUE** | | | | | | | | |
| 10/05/2016 | 12421 | 18.00 | 09/06/2016 | 18.00 | 18.00 | | | |
| 30/04/2016 | Inv W/032 | 970.80 | 30/05/2016 | 970.80 | | 970.80 | | |
| | | | | £988.80 | £18.00 | £970.80 | £0.00 | £0.00 |
| | | | TOTAL | £3,034.80 | £1,758.00 | £1,276.80 | £0.00 | £0.00 |

## TASK 11

### Aged Debtors Report

Toy Shop

| | | | | Toy Shop | | | | |
|---|---|---|---|---|---|---|---|---|
| To: 31/05/2016 | | | | **Aged Debtors Breakdown** | | | 20 Apr 2017 | 15:43 |
| Date | Reference | Total | Due Date | O/S Amt | < 30 days | < 60 days | < 90 days | Older |
| **Busy Bee Toys (BB01)**, Credit limit: £4,000.00 | | | | | | | | |
| , Terms: 30 days - OVERDUE | | | | | | | | |
| 04/05/2016 | QE-Inv 2021 | 3,102.00 | 03/06/2016 | 3,102.00 | 3,102.00 | | | |
| | | | | £3,102.00 | £3,102.00 | £0.00 | £0.00 | £0.00 |
| **Forming Fun (FF02)**, Credit limit: £4,000.00 | | | | | | | | |
| , Terms: 30 days - OVERDUE | | | | | | | | |
| 04/05/2016 | QE-Inv 2022 | 600.00 | 03/06/2016 | 600.00 | 600.00 | | | |
| | | | | £600.00 | £600.00 | £0.00 | £0.00 | £0.00 |
| **Space Models (SM03)**, Credit limit: £3,000.00 | | | | | | | | |
| , Terms: 30 days - OVERDUE | | | | | | | | |
| 30/04/2016 | OB-Inv 093 | 1,195.20 | 30/05/2016 | 1,195.20 | | 1,195.20 | | |
| | | | | £1,195.20 | £0.00 | £1,195.20 | £0.00 | £0.00 |
| **Teddy T's Party (TP04)**, Credit limit: £7,000.00 | | | | | | | | |
| , Terms: 30 days - OVERDUE | | | | | | | | |
| 06/05/2016 | QE-Inv 2023 | 6,000.00 | 05/06/2016 | 6,000.00 | 6,000.00 | | | |
| | | | | £6,000.00 | £6,000.00 | £0.00 | £0.00 | £0.00 |
| | | | TOTAL | £10,897.20 | £9,702.00 | £1,195.20 | £0.00 | £0.00 |

## TASK 12

### Customer address screen shot

**Forming Fun (Customer)** ✏️
Ref: FF02

| | | | |
|---|---|---|---|
| OUTSTANDING [1] | OVERDUE [1] | SALES TO DATE [2] | SALES THIS YEAR [0] |
| £600.00 | £600.00 | £699.60 | £0.00 |
| CREDIT LIMIT | CREDIT TERMS | LAST SALE | AVERAGE SALE |
| £4,000.00 | 30 Days | 04 May 2016 | £349.80 |

👤 Main Contact
📍 100 Aventi Way, St Albans, AL2 4PM

Activity | Contacts and Addresses | Payment Details | Options | Notes

**Invoice Address** MAIN ✏️
Sales

100 Aventi Way
St Albans
Hertfordshire
AL2 4PM
United Kingdom (GB)

**Main Contact** MAIN ✏️

New Contact +

## TASK 14

Remittance Advices

# Remittance Advice

Date Paid: 28/05/2016

Reference: PL03

**Space Models**
13 Central Street
Perth
Scotland

**Toy Shop**
64 Long Lane
Langhorne
North Yorkshire
YO21 3EJ
United Kingdom

Telephone: 01234 567891

VAT Number: GB 123456789

**Reference:** Chq no 101335

| Our Ref | Your Ref | Date | Total Amount | Amount Paid |
|---|---|---|---|---|
| Inv F-0193 | | 30/04/2016 | 306.00 | 306.00 |
| | | **Total Paid:** | | **£ 306.00 GBP** |

**TASK 14**

Remittance Advices

# Remittance Advice

Date Paid: 28/05/2016

Reference: PL04

| Toys Unlimited 95 Cuscaden Road Edinburgh Scotland | **Toy Shop** 64 Long Lane Langhorne North Yorkshire YO21 3EJ United Kingdom |
|---|---|
| | Telephone: 01234 567891 |
| | VAT Number: GB 123456789 |

**Reference:** Chq no 101336

| Our Ref | Your Ref | Date | Total Amount | Amount Paid |
|---|---|---|---|---|
| Inv W/032 | | 30/04/2016 | 970.80 | 450.00 |
| | | | **Total Paid:** | **£ 450.00 GBP** |

**TASK 14**

Remittance Advices

# Remittance Advice

Date Paid: 28/05/2016

Reference: PL01

| Abacus C & C Unit 31 Kitts Industrial Estate St Helens Lancs | **Toy Shop** 64 Long Lane Langhorne North Yorkshire YO21 3EJ United Kingdom |
|---|---|
| | Telephone: 01234 567891 |
| | VAT Number: GB 123456789 |

**Reference:** BACS

| Our Ref | Your Ref | Date | Total Amount | Amount Paid |
|---|---|---|---|---|
| B/989 | | 03/05/2016 | 540.00 | 540.00 |
| | | | **Total Paid:** | **£ 540.00 GBP** |

## TASK 18

Recurring payment

## TASK 22

### Customer Activity (detailed) Report

**Busy Bee Toys (BB01)**

| Date | Number | Reference | Type | Net | VAT | Total | Discount | Outstanding |
|---|---|---|---|---|---|---|---|---|
| 30/04/2016 | | Inv 021 | Customer OB Invoice | 349.20 | 0.00 | 349.20 | | 0.00 |
| 04/05/2016 | | Inv 2021 | Sales QE Invoice | 2,585.00 | 517.00 | 3,102.00 | | 0.00 |
| 17/05/2016 | | Chq no 100322 | Customer Receipt | | | -349.20 | 0.00 | 0.00 |
| 29/05/2016 | | | Customer Receipt | | | -3,102.00 | 0.00 | 0.00 |
| | | | | | | **0.00** | | **0.00** |

**Forming Fun (FF02)**

| Date | Number | Reference | Type | Net | VAT | Total | Discount | Outstanding |
|---|---|---|---|---|---|---|---|---|
| 30/04/2016 | | Inv 035 | Customer OB Invoice | 99.60 | 0.00 | 99.60 | | 0.00 |
| 04/05/2016 | | Inv 2022 | Sales QE Invoice | 500.00 | 100.00 | 600.00 | | 200.00 |
| 17/05/2016 | | Chq no 267543 | Customer Receipt | | | -99.60 | 0.00 | 0.00 |
| 29/05/2016 | | Chq no 828100 | Customer Receipt | | | -400.00 | 0.00 | 0.00 |
| | | | | | | **200.00** | | **200.00** |

**Space Models (SM03)**

| Date | Number | Reference | Type | Net | VAT | Total | Discount | Outstanding |
|---|---|---|---|---|---|---|---|---|
| 30/04/2016 | | Inv 093 | Customer OB Invoice | 1,195.20 | 0.00 | 1,195.20 | | 1,195.20 |
| | | | | | | **1,195.20** | | **1,195.20** |

**Teddy T's Party (TP04)**

| Date | Number | Reference | Type | Net | VAT | Total | Discount | Outstanding |
|---|---|---|---|---|---|---|---|---|
| 30/04/2016 | | Inv 1003 | Customer OB Invoice | 579.60 | 0.00 | 579.60 | | 0.00 |
| 06/05/2016 | | Inv 2023 | Sales QE Invoice | 5,000.00 | 1,000.00 | 6,000.00 | | 0.00 |
| 13/05/2016 | | CN101 | Sales QE Credit | -320.00 | -64.00 | -384.00 | | 0.00 |
| 26/05/2016 | | BACS | Customer Receipt | | | -195.60 | 0.00 | 0.00 |
| 29/05/2016 | | Chq no 672522 | Customer Receipt | | | -6,000.00 | 0.00 | 0.00 |
| | | | | | | **0.00** | | **0.00** |

## TASK 22

### Supplier Activity (detailed) Report

**Abacus C & C (PL01)**

| Date | Number | Reference | Type | Net | VAT | Total | Discount | Outstanding |
|------|--------|-----------|------|-----|-----|-------|----------|-------------|
| 30/04/2016 | | Inv B/1874 | Supplier OB Invoice | 369.60 | 0.00 | 369.60 | | 0.00 |
| 03/05/2016 | | B/989 | Purchase QE Invoice | 450.00 | 90.00 | 540.00 | | 0.00 |
| 22/05/2016 | | Chq no 101333 | Supplier Payment | | | -369.60 | 0.00 | 0.00 |
| 28/05/2016 | | BACS | Supplier Payment | | | -540.00 | 0.00 | 0.00 |
| | | | | | | 0.00 | | 0.00 |

**Compugames Ltd (PL02)**

| Date | Number | Reference | Type | Net | VAT | Total | Discount | Outstanding |
|------|--------|-----------|------|-----|-----|-------|----------|-------------|
| 30/04/2016 | | Inv 1087 | Supplier OB Invoice | 511.20 | 0.00 | 511.20 | | 0.00 |
| 05/05/2016 | | 145215 | Purchase QE Invoice | 500.00 | 100.00 | 600.00 | | 0.00 |
| 15/05/2016 | | CR 11245 | Purchase QE Credit | -88.00 | -17.60 | -105.60 | | 0.00 |
| 22/05/2016 | | Chq no 101334 | Supplier Payment | | | -1,005.60 | 0.00 | 0.00 |
| | | | | | | 0.00 | | 0.00 |

**Space Models (PL03)**

| Date | Number | Reference | Type | Net | VAT | Total | Discount | Outstanding |
|------|--------|-----------|------|-----|-----|-------|----------|-------------|
| 30/04/2016 | | Inv F-0193 | Supplier OB Invoice | 306.00 | 0.00 | 306.00 | | 0.00 |
| 10/05/2016 | | C-32632 | Purchase QE Invoice | 1,000.00 | 200.00 | 1,200.00 | | 1,200.00 |
| 28/05/2016 | | Chq no 101335 | Supplier Payment | | | -306.00 | 0.00 | 0.00 |
| | | | | | | 1,200.00 | | 1,200.00 |

**Toys Unlimited (PL04)**

| Date | Number | Reference | Type | Net | VAT | Total | Discount | Outstanding |
|------|--------|-----------|------|-----|-----|-------|----------|-------------|
| 30/04/2016 | | Inv W/032 | Supplier OB Invoice | 970.80 | 0.00 | 970.80 | | 520.80 |
| 10/05/2016 | | 12421 | Purchase QE Invoice | 18.00 | 0.00 | 18.00 | | 18.00 |
| 28/05/2016 | | Chq no 101336 | Supplier Payment | | | -450.00 | 0.00 | 0.00 |
| | | | | | | 538.80 | | 538.80 |

## TASK 22

## Period Trial Balance for May

From: 30/04/2016
To:    31/05/2016

Toy Shop
**Trial Balance Report**

21 Apr 2017
11:05

This period only

| Nominal Code | Name | Selected Period | |
|---|---|---|---|
| | | Debit | Credit |
| 0040 | Fixtures and fittings - Cost | 5,800.00 | |
| 0050 | Motor Vehicles - Cost | 3,000.00 | |
| 1100 | Trade Debtors | 1,395.20 | |
| 1200 | Current | 24,337.80 | |
| 1210 | Cash | 300.00 | |
| 1220 | Deposit | 500.00 | |
| 2100 | Trade Creditors | | 1,738.80 |
| 2200 | VAT on Sales | | 2,819.90 |
| 2201 | VAT on Purchases | 483.48 | |
| 2500 | Loan | | 10,000.00 |
| 3200 | Capital introduced | | 20,000.00 |
| 3260 | Drawings - equity | 2,355.00 | |
| 4000 | Sales - Computer Games | | 15,560.00 |
| 4001 | Sales - Jigsaws | | 3,144.50 |
| 4002 | Sales - Boxed Games | | 2,467.00 |
| 5000 | Purchases - Computer Games | 9,362.00 | |
| 5001 | Purchases - Jigsaws | 3,218.00 | |
| 5002 | Purchases - Boxed Games | 2,965.00 | |
| 7100 | Rent and rates | 1,048.00 | |
| 7200 | Electricity | 669.00 | |
| 7500 | Office Stationery | 53.00 | |
| 7610 | Insurance | 100.00 | |
| 7900 | Bank charges and interest | 101.32 | |
| 8201 | Subscriptions | 32.00 | |
| 8205 | Refreshments | 10.40 | |
| | TOTAL | £55,730.20 | £55,730.20 |

## TASK 22

### Audit Trail for May (detailed – transactions only including bank reconciled)

From: 30/04/2016
To: 31/05/2016

Toy Shop
**Audit Trail Breakdown**

21 Apr 2017
11:06

Type: All, Status: All

| Trx No | Entry Date | User | Trx Date | Name | Type | Invoice Number | Ref | Ledger Account | Debit | Credit | Bank Reconciled |
|---|---|---|---|---|---|---|---|---|---|---|---|
| 1 | 20/04/2017 | LH | 30/04/2016 | Busy Bee Toys (BB01) | Customer OB Invoice | | Inv 021 | Opening Balances Control Account (9998) | | 349.20 | No |
| | | | | | | | | Trade Debtors (1100) | 349.20 | | No |
| 2 | 20/04/2017 | LH | 30/04/2016 | Forming Fun (FF02) | Customer OB Invoice | | Inv 035 | Opening Balances Control Account (9998) | | 99.60 | No |
| | | | | | | | | Trade Debtors (1100) | 99.60 | | No |
| 3 | 20/04/2017 | LH | 30/04/2016 | Space Models (SM03) | Customer OB Invoice | | Inv 093 | Opening Balances Control Account (9998) | | 1,195.20 | No |
| | | | | | | | | Trade Debtors (1100) | 1,195.20 | | No |
| 4 | 20/04/2017 | LH | 30/04/2016 | Teddy T's Party (TP04) | Customer OB Invoice | | Inv 1003 | Opening Balances Control Account (9998) | | 579.60 | No |
| | | | | | | | | Trade Debtors (1100) | 579.60 | | No |
| 5 | 20/04/2017 | LH | 30/04/2016 | Abacus C & C (PL01) | Supplier OB Invoice | | Inv B/1874 | Trade Creditors (2100) | | 369.60 | No |
| | | | | | | | | Opening Balances Control Account (9998) | 369.60 | | No |
| 6 | 20/04/2017 | LH | 30/04/2016 | Compugames Ltd (PL02) | Supplier OB Invoice | | Inv 1087 | Trade Creditors (2100) | | 511.20 | No |
| | | | | | | | | Opening Balances Control Account (9998) | 511.20 | | No |
| 7 | 20/04/2017 | LH | 30/04/2016 | Space Models (PL03) | Supplier OB Invoice | | Inv F-0193 | Trade Creditors (2100) | | 306.00 | No |
| | | | | | | | | Opening Balances Control Account (9998) | 306.00 | | No |
| 8 | 20/04/2017 | LH | 30/04/2016 | Toys Unlimited (PL04) | Supplier OB Invoice | | Inv W/032 | Trade Creditors (2100) | | 970.80 | No |
| | | | | | | | | Opening Balances Control Account (9998) | 970.80 | | No |
| 9 | 20/04/2017 | LH | 30/04/2016 | | Bank Opening Balance | | | Opening Balances Control Account (9998) | | 4,225.00 | No |
| | | | | | | | | Current (1200) | 4,225.00 | | Yes |
| 10 | 20/04/2017 | LH | 30/04/2016 | | Bank Opening Balance | | | Opening Balances Control Account (9998) | | 300.00 | No |
| | | | | | | | | Cash (1210) | 300.00 | | No |
| 12 | 20/04/2017 | LH | 30/04/2016 | | Journal Opening Balance | | OB 1/5/16 | VAT on Sales (2200) | | 543.00 | No |
| | | | | | | | | Opening Balances Control Account (9998) | 543.00 | | No |

From: 30/04/2016
To: 31/05/2016

Toy Shop
**Audit Trail Breakdown**

21 Apr 2017
11:06

| | | | | | | | | Ledger Account | Debit | Credit | Bank Reconciled |
|---|---|---|---|---|---|---|---|---|---|---|---|
| | | | | | | | | VAT on Purchases (2201) | 109.00 | | No |
| | | | | | | | | Opening Balances Control Account (9998) | | 109.00 | No |
| | | | | | | | | Capital introduced (3200) | | 20,000.00 | No |
| | | | | | | | | Opening Balances Control Account (9998) | 20,000.00 | | No |
| | | | | | | | | Drawings - equity (3260) | 355.00 | | No |
| | | | | | | | | Opening Balances Control Account (9998) | | 355.00 | No |
| | | | | | | | | Sales - Computer Games (4000) | | 6,080.00 | No |
| | | | | | | | | Opening Balances Control Account (9998) | 6,080.00 | | No |
| | | | | | | | | Sales - Jigsaws (4001) | | 700.00 | No |
| | | | | | | | | Opening Balances Control Account (9998) | 700.00 | | No |
| | | | | | | | | Sales - Boxed Games (4002) | | 1,967.00 | No |
| | | | | | | | | Opening Balances Control Account (9998) | 1,967.00 | | No |
| | | | | | | | | Purchases - Computer Games (5000) | 8,000.00 | | No |
| | | | | | | | | Opening Balances Control Account (9998) | | 8,000.00 | No |
| | | | | | | | | Purchases - Jigsaws (5001) | 3,200.00 | | No |
| | | | | | | | | Opening Balances Control Account (9998) | | 3,200.00 | No |
| | | | | | | | | Purchases - Boxed Games (5002) | 2,465.00 | | No |
| | | | | | | | | Opening Balances Control Account (9998) | | 2,465.00 | No |
| | | | | | | | | Office Stationery (7500) | 53.00 | | No |
| | | | | | | | | Opening Balances Control Account (9998) | | 53.00 | No |
| | | | | | | | | Electricity (7200) | 167.00 | | No |
| | | | | | | | | Opening Balances Control Account (9998) | | 167.00 | No |
| | | | | | | | | Rent and rates (7100) | 1,550.00 | | No |
| | | | | | | | | Opening Balances Control Account (9998) | | 1,550.00 | No |
| | | | | | | | | Fixtures and fittings - Cost (0040) | 5,800.00 | | No |
| | | | | | | | | Opening Balances Control Account (9998) | | 5,800.00 | No |

From: 30/04/2016
To: 31/05/2016

Toy Shop
**Audit Trail Breakdown**

21 Apr 2017
11:06

| No | Date | User | Trans Date | Name | Type | Ref | Account | Debit | Credit | Paid |
|---|---|---|---|---|---|---|---|---|---|---|
| | | | | | | | Motor Vehicles - Cost (0050) | 3,000.00 | | No |
| | | | | | | | Opening Balances Control Account (9998) | | 3,000.00 | No |
| 13 | 20/04/2017 | LH | 01/05/2016 | | Bank Transfer | TRANS01 | Current (1200) | | 500.00 | Yes |
| | | | | | | | Deposit (1220) | 500.00 | | No |
| 14 | 20/04/2017 | LH | 04/05/2016 | Busy Bee Toys (BB01) | Sales QE Invoice | Inv 2021 | Sales - Computer Games (4000) | | 2,585.00 | No |
| | | | | | | | VAT on Sales (2200) | | 517.00 | No |
| | | | | | | | Trade Debtors (1100) | 3,102.00 | | No |
| 15 | 20/04/2017 | LH | 04/05/2016 | Forming Fun (FF02) | Sales QE Invoice | Inv 2022 | Sales - Boxed Games (4002) | | 500.00 | No |
| | | | | | | | VAT on Sales (2200) | | 100.00 | No |
| | | | | | | | Trade Debtors (1100) | 600.00 | | No |
| 16 | 20/04/2017 | LH | 06/05/2016 | Teddy T's Party (TP04) | Sales QE Invoice | Inv 2023 | Sales - Computer Games (4000) | | 5,000.00 | No |
| | | | | | | | VAT on Sales (2200) | | 1,000.00 | No |
| | | | | | | | Trade Debtors (1100) | 6,000.00 | | No |
| 17 | 20/04/2017 | LH | 13/05/2016 | Teddy T's Party (TP04) | Sales QE Credit | CN101 | Trade Debtors (1100) | | 384.00 | No |
| | | | | | | | Sales - Computer Games (4000) | 320.00 | | No |
| | | | | | | | VAT on Sales (2200) | 64.00 | | No |
| 18 | 20/04/2017 | LH | 03/05/2016 | Abacus C & C (PL01) | Purchase QE Invoice | B/989 | Trade Creditors (2100) | | 540.00 | No |
| | | | | | | | Purchases - Computer Games (5000) | 450.00 | | No |
| | | | | | | | VAT on Purchases (2201) | 90.00 | | No |
| 19 | 20/04/2017 | LH | 05/05/2016 | Compugames Ltd (PL02) | Purchase QE Invoice | 145215 | Trade Creditors (2100) | | 600.00 | No |
| | | | | | | | Purchases - Boxed Games (5002) | 500.00 | | No |
| | | | | | | | VAT on Purchases (2201) | 100.00 | | No |
| 20 | 20/04/2017 | LH | 10/05/2016 | Space Models (PL03) | Purchase QE Invoice | C-32632 | Trade Creditors (2100) | | 1,200.00 | No |
| | | | | | | | Purchases - Computer Games (5000) | 1,000.00 | | No |
| | | | | | | | VAT on Purchases (2201) | 200.00 | | No |
| 22 | 20/04/2017 | LH | 15/05/2016 | Compugames Ltd (PL02) | Purchase QE Credit | CR 11245 | Purchases - Computer Games (5000) | | 88.00 | No |
| | | | | | | | VAT on Purchases (2201) | | 17.60 | No |
| | | | | | | | Trade Creditors (2100) | 105.60 | | No |
| 23 | 20/04/2017 | LH | 17/05/2016 | Busy Bee Toys (BB01) | Customer Receipt | Chq no 100322 | Trade Debtors (1100) | | 349.20 | No |
| | | | | | | | Current (1200) | 349.20 | | Yes |
| 24 | 20/04/2017 | LH | 17/05/2016 | Forming Fun (FF02) | Customer Receipt | Chq no 267543 | Trade Debtors (1100) | | 99.60 | No |
| | | | | | | | Current (1200) | 99.60 | | Yes |
| 25 | 20/04/2017 | LH | 26/05/2016 | Teddy T's Party (TP04) | Customer Receipt | BACS | Trade Debtors (1100) | | 579.60 | No |
| | | | | | | | Trade Debtors (1100) | 384.00 | | No |
| | | | | | | | Current (1200) | 195.60 | | Yes |
| 26 | 20/04/2017 | LH | 22/05/2016 | Abacus C & C (PL01) | Supplier Payment | Chq no 101333 | Trade Creditors (2100) | 369.60 | | No |
| | | | | | | | Current (1200) | | 369.60 | Yes |
| 27 | 20/04/2017 | LH | 22/05/2016 | Compuganes Ltd (PL02) | Supplier Payment | Chq no 101334 | Trade Creditors (2100) | 511.20 | | No |
| | | | | | | | Trade Creditors (2100) | 600.00 | | No |
| | | | | | | | Trade Creditors (2100) | | 105.60 | No |
| | | | | | | | Current (1200) | | 1,005.60 | Yes |
| 28 | 20/04/2017 | LH | 13/05/2016 | | Other Receipt | Cash sale | Sales - Computer Games (4000) | | 1,000.00 | No |
| | | | | | | | VAT on Sales (2200) | | 200.00 | No |
| | | | | | | | Current (1200) | 1,200.00 | | Yes |
| 29 | 20/04/2017 | LH | 13/05/2016 | | Other Receipt | Cash sale | Sales - Jigsaws (4001) | | 2,399.50 | No |
| | | | | | | | VAT on Sales (2200) | | 479.90 | No |
| | | | | | | | Current (1200) | 2,879.40 | | Yes |
| 30 | 20/04/2017 | LH | 20/05/2016 | | Other Receipt | Cash sale | Sales - Computer Games (4000) | | 995.00 | No |
| | | | | | | | Current (1200) | 995.00 | | Yes |
| 31 | 20/04/2017 | LH | 20/05/2016 | | Other Payment | Voucher 012 | Cash (1210) | | 32.00 | No |
| | | | | | | | Subscriptions (8201) | 32.00 | | No |
| 32 | 20/04/2017 | LH | 21/05/2016 | | Other Payment | Voucher 013 | Cash (1210) | | 12.48 | No |
| | | | | | | | Refreshments (8205) | 10.40 | | No |
| | | | | | | | VAT on Purchases (2201) | 2.08 | | No |

| | | | | | | | | | | |
|---|---|---|---|---|---|---|---|---|---|---|
| 33 | 20/04/2017 | LH | 25/05/2016 | | Journal | JNL02 | Drawings - equity (3260) | 2,000.00 | | No |
| | | | | | | | Current (1200) | | 2,000.00 | Yes |
| 34 | 20/04/2017 | LH | 10/05/2016 | Toys Unlimited (PL04) | Purchase QE Invoice | 12421 | Trade Creditors (2100) | | 18.00 | No |
| | | | | | | | Purchases - Jigsaws (5001) | 18.00 | | No |
| 35 | 20/04/2017 | LH | 31/05/2016 | | Journal | JNL03 | Electricity (7200) | 502.00 | | No |
| | | | | | | | Rent and rates (7100) | | 502.00 | No |
| 36 | 20/04/2017 | LH | 28/05/2016 | Space Models (PL03) | Supplier Payment | Chq no 101335 | Trade Creditors (2100) | 306.00 | | No |
| | | | | | | | Current (1200) | | 306.00 | No |
| 37 | 20/04/2017 | LH | 28/05/2016 | Toys Unlimited (PL04) | Supplier Payment | Chq no 101336 | Trade Creditors (2100) | 450.00 | | No |
| | | | | | | | Current (1200) | | 450.00 | Yes |
| 38 | 20/04/2017 | LH | 28/05/2016 | Abacus C & C (PL01) | Supplier Payment | BACS | Trade Creditors (2100) | 540.00 | | No |
| | | | | | | | Current (1200) | | 540.00 | Yes |
| 39 | 20/04/2017 | LH | 29/05/2016 | Busy Bee Toys (BB01) | Customer Receipt | | Trade Debtors (1100) | | 3,102.00 | No |
| | | | | | | | Current (1200) | 3,102.00 | | Yes |
| 40 | 20/04/2017 | LH | 29/05/2016 | Forming Fun (FF02) | Customer Receipt | Chq no 826100 | Trade Debtors (1100) | | 400.00 | No |
| | | | | | | | Current (1200) | 400.00 | | Yes |
| 41 | 20/04/2017 | LH | 29/05/2016 | Teddy T's Party (TP04) | Customer Receipt | Chq no 672522 | Trade Debtors (1100) | | 6,000.00 | No |
| | | | | | | | Current (1200) | 6,000.00 | | Yes |
| 42 | 20/04/2017 | LH | 14/05/2016 | | Other Receipt | CSH41 | Sales - Computer Games (4000) | | 220.00 | No |
| | | | | | | | VAT on Sales (2200) | | 44.00 | No |
| | | | | | | | Current (1200) | 264.00 | | Yes |
| 43 | 20/04/2017 | LH | 19/05/2016 | | Other Receipt | Debit card | Sales - Jigsaws (4001) | | 45.00 | No |
| | | | | | | | VAT on Sales (2200) | | | No |
| | | | | | | | Current (1200) | 45.00 | | Yes |
| 46 | 20/04/2017 | LH | 31/05/2016 | | Other Payment | Direct Debit Insurance | Current (1200) | | 100.00 | Yes |
| | | | | | | | Insurance (7610) | 100.00 | | No |
| | | | | | | | VAT on Purchases (2201) | | | No |
| 57 | 20/04/2017 | LH | 31/05/2016 | | Journal | JNL04 | Current (1200) | 10,000.00 | | Yes |
| | | | | | | | Loan (2500) | | 10,000.00 | No |
| 58 | 21/04/2017 | LH | 31/05/2016 | | Bank Transfer | CSH25 | Current (1200) | | 44.48 | Yes |
| | | | | | | | Cash (1210) | 44.48 | | No |
| 59 | 21/04/2017 | LH | 31/05/2016 | | Bank Payment | Bank Charge | Current (1200) | | 101.32 | Yes |
| | | | | | | | Bank charges and interest (7900) | 101.32 | | No |

## TASK 22

### Aged Debtors (summary)

To: 31/05/2016

Toy Shop
**Aged Debtors Report**

21 Apr 2017
11:16

| Customer | Credit limit | O/S Amt | < 30 days | < 60 days | < 90 days | Older |
|---|---|---|---|---|---|---|
| Forming Fun (FF02) | £4,000.00 | £200.00 | £200.00 | £0.00 | £0.00 | £0.00 |
| Space Models (SM03) | £3,000.00 | £1,195.20 | £0.00 | £1,195.20 | £0.00 | £0.00 |
| TOTAL | | £1,395.20 | £200.00 | £1,195.20 | £0.00 | £0.00 |

## PRACTICE PAPER 2

## CRAZY HAIR ANSWERS

### TASK 3.2

**Customer Address List**

| | | Crazy Hair<br>**Customer Address List** | | | | 21 Apr 2017<br>12:06 |
|---|---|---|---|---|---|---|

Address Types: All

| Customer Name | Address | Contact name | Phone | Mobile | Email | Fax |
|---|---|---|---|---|---|---|
| Alfred Images (104) | Masuki Offices<br>PO Box 5684<br>Birmingham<br>B23 4RD | Main Contact | | | | |
| Figgaro (110) | Beta Studio<br>34 Knightsbridge Way<br>Morden<br>SE23 4KA | Main Contact | | | | |
| Blades (118) | Alpha Studio<br>45 Key West<br>London<br>SE1 0JF | Main Contact | | | | |
| Hair Studio (122) | Framlington Court<br>Lee<br>London<br>SE4 7YH | Main Contact | | | | |
| Ribbons & Curls (138) | PO Box 1120<br>Canning Town<br>London<br>TN2 2EB | Main Contact | | | | |

### TASK 3.2

**Supplier Address List**

| | | Crazy Hair<br>**Supplier Address List** | | | | 21 Apr 2017<br>12:12 |
|---|---|---|---|---|---|---|

Address Types: All

| Supplier Name | Address | Contact name | Phone | Mobile | Email | Fax |
|---|---|---|---|---|---|---|
| Avada Cash & Carry (1134) | 32 Surrey Quay<br>Isle of Dogs<br>E12 3NW | Main Contact | | | | |
| Straightside Supplies (1138) | Havering Place<br>Holborn<br>London<br>WC1 2PP | Main Contact | | | | |
| Hair Supplies (1165) | 43 St Helens Way<br>London<br>SE7 3RF | Main Contact | | | | |
| Wig Specialists (1185) | Retro Square<br>32 Wigmore Road<br>London<br>EC1V 3SG | Main Contact | | | | |

## TASK 3.2

### Trial Balance

| From: 30/04/2016 | Crazy Hair | 21 Apr 2017 |
|---|---|---|
| To: 31/05/2016 | **Trial Balance Report** | 12:18 |

This period only

| Nominal Code | Name | Selected Period | |
|---|---|---|---|
| | | Debit | Credit |
| 0040 | Fixtures and fittings - Cost | 31,000.00 | |
| 0050 | Motor Vehicles - Cost | 24,000.00 | |
| 1100 | Trade Debtors | 8,907.60 | |
| 1200 | Current | 54,210.81 | |
| 1210 | Petty Cash | 200.00 | |
| 2100 | Trade Creditors | | 7,214.40 |
| 2200 | VAT on Sales | | 5,550.00 |
| 2201 | VAT on Purchases | 1,507.94 | |
| 3200 | Capital introduced | | 165,000.00 |
| 3260 | Drawings - equity | 5,000.00 | |
| 4000 | Sales - Brushes | | 345.00 |
| 4001 | Sales - Combs | | 187.00 |
| 4002 | Sales - Colours | | 3,801.45 |
| 4003 | Sales - Hairdryers | | 758.00 |
| 4004 | Sales - Wigs | | 5,600.00 |
| 4005 | Cash Sales | | 617.50 |
| 5000 | Purchases - Brushes | 873.00 | |
| 5001 | Purchases - Combs | 50.00 | |
| 5002 | Purchases - Colour | 4,200.00 | |
| 5003 | Purchases - Hairdryers | 6,310.00 | |
| 5004 | Purchases - Wigs | 52,814.00 | |
| | TOTAL | £189,073.35 | £189,073.35 |

## TASK 9

Remittance advices

# Remittance Advice

Date Paid: 31/05/2016

Reference: 1185

**Wigs Specialist**
Retro Square
32 Wigmore Road
London
EC1V 3SG

**Crazy Hair**
34 Clapham Road
Clapham
London
SE3 2HR
United Kingdom

Telephone: 01234 567891

VAT Number: GB 123456789

**Reference:** Chq no 163455

| Our Ref | Your Ref | Date | Total Amount | Amount Paid |
|---------|----------|------|--------------|-------------|
| Inv S653 | | 30/04/2016 | 102.00 | 102.00 |
| | | | **Total Paid:** | **£ 102.00 GBP** |

# Remittance Advice

Date Paid: 31/05/2016

Reference: 1134

**Avada Cash & Carry**
32 Surrey Quay
Isle of Dogs
E12 3NW

**Crazy Hair**
34 Clapham Road
Clapham
London
SE3 2HR
United Kingdom

Telephone: 01234 567891

VAT Number: GB 123456789

**Reference:** Chq No 163456

| Our Ref | Your Ref | Date | Total Amount | Amount Paid |
|---------|----------|------|--------------|-------------|
| Inv C/251 | | 30/04/2016 | 4,454.40 | 4,454.40 |
| | | | **Total Paid:** | **£ 4,454.40 GBP** |

# Remittance Advice

Date Paid: 31/05/2016

Reference: 1165

**Hair Supplies**
43 St Helens Way
London
SE7 3RF

**Crazy Hair**
34 Clapham Road
Clapham
London
SE3 2HR
United Kingdom

Telephone: 01234 567891

VAT Number: GB 123456789

**Reference:** Chq no 163457

| Our Ref | Your Ref | Date | Total Amount | Amount Paid |
|---------|----------|------|--------------|-------------|
| Inv 0028 | | 30/04/2016 | 818.40 | 818.40 |
| | | | **Total Paid:** | **£ 818.40 GBP** |

## TASK 12

### Trial Balance

| From: 30/04/2016 | Crazy Hair | 24 Apr 2017 |
| To: 31/05/2016 | **Trial Balance Report** | 13:32 |

This period only

| Nominal Code | Name | Selected Period | |
| --- | --- | --- | --- |
| | | Debit | Credit |
| 0040 | Fixtures and fittings – Cost | 31,000.00 | |
| 0050 | Motor Vehicles – Cost | 24,000.00 | |
| 1100 | Trade Debtors | 5,964.33 | |
| 1200 | Current | 57,373.41 | |
| 1210 | Petty Cash | 155.17 | |
| 2100 | Trade Creditors | | 7,341.96 |
| 2200 | VAT on Sales | | 6,482.35 |
| 2201 | VAT on Purchases | 2,401.96 | |
| 3200 | Capital introduced | | 165,000.00 |
| 3260 | Drawings – equity | 5,000.00 | |
| 4000 | Sales – Brushes | | 1,204.30 |
| 4001 | Sales – Combs | | 187.00 |
| 4002 | Sales – Colours | | 4,172.85 |
| 4003 | Sales – Hairdryers | | 1,621.40 |
| 4004 | Sales – Wigs | | 8,167.68 |
| 4005 | Cash Sales | | 617.50 |
| 5000 | Purchases – Brushes | 1,064.60 | |
| 5001 | Purchases – Combs | 50.00 | |
| 5002 | Purchases – Colour | 5,154.00 | |
| 5003 | Purchases – Hairdryers | 6,488.56 | |
| 5004 | Purchases – Wigs | 56,104.90 | |
| 7400 | Travel and Entertainment | 33.60 | |
| 7500 | Office costs | 4.51 | |
| | TOTAL | £194,795.04 | £194,795.04 |

## TASK 12

### Sales Day Book

| From: 30/04/2016<br>To: 31/05/2016 | | | Crazy Hair<br>**Sales Day Book Report** | | | | | 24 Apr 2017<br>13:34 | |
| --- | --- | --- | --- | --- | --- | --- | --- | --- | --- |

Type: Sales QE Invoice

| Trx No | Type | Date | Name | Invoice Number | Ref | Details | Net | VAT | Total |
| --- | --- | --- | --- | --- | --- | --- | --- | --- | --- |
| 13 | Sales QE Invoice | 12/05/2016 | Ribbons & Curls | | Inv 3353 | | 141.00 | 28.20 | 169.20 |
| 14 | Sales QE Invoice | 12/05/2016 | Alfred Images | | Inv 3354 | | 581.00 | 116.20 | 697.20 |
| 15 | Sales QE Invoice | 13/05/2016 | Figgaro | | Inv 3355 | | 660.00 | 132.00 | 792.00 |
| 16 | Sales QE Invoice | 15/05/2016 | Blades | | Inv 3356 | | 1,685.76 | 337.15 | 2,022.91 |
| 17 | Sales QE Invoice | 15/05/2016 | Blades | | Inv 3356 | | 203.40 | 40.68 | 244.08 |
| 18 | Sales QE Invoice | 18/05/2016 | Hair Studio | | Inv 3357 | | 316.80 | 63.36 | 380.16 |
| 19 | Sales QE Invoice | 18/05/2016 | Hair Studio | | Inv 3357 | | 881.92 | 176.38 | 1,058.30 |
| 20 | Sales QE Invoice | 18/05/2016 | Hair Studio | | Inv 3357 | | 230.40 | 46.08 | 276.48 |
| | | | | | | TOTAL | £4,700.28 | £940.05 | £5,640.33 |

## TASK 12

### Sales Returns Day Book

| From: 30/04/2016<br>To: 31/05/2016 | | | Crazy Hair<br>**Sales Day Book Report** | | | | | 24 Apr 2017<br>13:35 | |
| --- | --- | --- | --- | --- | --- | --- | --- | --- | --- |

Type: Sales QE Credit

| Trx No | Type | Date | Name | Invoice Number | Ref | Details | Net | VAT | Total |
| --- | --- | --- | --- | --- | --- | --- | --- | --- | --- |
| 21 | Sales QE Credit | 25/05/2016 | Alfred Images | | CN23 | | -56.00 | -11.20 | -67.20 |
| | | | | | | TOTAL | -£56.00 | -£11.20 | -£67.20 |

## TASK 12

### Purchase Day Book

From: 30/04/2016
To: 31/05/2016

**Crazy Hair**
**Purchase Day Book Report**

24 Apr 2017
13:36

Type: Purchase QE Invoice

| Trx No | Type | Date | Name | Invoice Number | Ref | Details | Net | VAT | Total |
|---|---|---|---|---|---|---|---|---|---|
| 22 | Purchase QE Invoice | 11/05/2016 | Straightside Supplies | | Inv 3362 | | 191.60 | 38.32 | 229.92 |
| 37 | Purchase QE Invoice | 11/05/2016 | Avada Cash & Carry | | Inv C/910 | | 954.00 | 190.80 | 1,144.80 |
| 24 | Purchase QE Invoice | 13/05/2016 | Hair Supplies | | Inv 0814 | | 178.56 | 0.00 | 178.56 |
| 25 | Purchase QE Invoice | 14/05/2016 | Wig Specialists | | Inv S1198 | | 3,393.60 | 678.72 | 4,072.32 |
| | | | | | | TOTAL | £4,717.76 | £907.84 | £5,625.60 |

## TASK 12

### Customer Activity Report

From: 30/04/2016
To: 31/05/2016

**Crazy Hair**
**Customer Activity Report**

24 Apr 2017
13:38

**Alfred Images (104)**

| Date | Number | Reference | Type | Net | VAT | Total | Discount | Outstanding |
|---|---|---|---|---|---|---|---|---|
| 30/04/2016 | | Inv 3352 | Customer OB Invoice | 1,809.60 | 0.00 | 1,809.60 | | 0.00 |
| 12/05/2016 | | Inv 3354 | Sales QE Invoice | 581.00 | 116.20 | 697.20 | | 697.20 |
| 20/05/2016 | | Cheque no 183001 | Customer Receipt | | | -1,809.60 | 0.00 | 0.00 |
| 25/05/2016 | | CN23 | Sales QE Credit | -56.00 | -11.20 | -67.20 | | -67.20 |
| | | | | | | 630.00 | | 630.00 |

**Figgaro (110)**

| Date | Number | Reference | Type | Net | VAT | Total | Discount | Outstanding |
|---|---|---|---|---|---|---|---|---|
| 30/04/2016 | | Inv 2856 | Customer OB Invoice | 3,880.80 | 0.00 | 3,880.80 | | 0.00 |
| 13/05/2016 | | Inv 3355 | Sales QE Invoice | 660.00 | 132.00 | 792.00 | | 792.00 |
| 21/05/2016 | | BACS | Customer Receipt | | | -3,880.80 | 0.00 | 0.00 |
| | | | | | | 792.00 | | 792.00 |

**Blades (118)**

| Date | Number | Reference | Type | Net | VAT | Total | Discount | Outstanding |
|---|---|---|---|---|---|---|---|---|
| 30/04/2016 | | Inv 3345 | Customer OB Invoice | 2,144.40 | 0.00 | 2,144.40 | | 0.00 |
| 15/05/2016 | | Inv 3356 | Sales QE Invoice | 1,685.76 | 337.15 | 2,022.91 | | 2,022.91 |
| 15/05/2016 | | Inv 3356 | Sales QE Invoice | 203.40 | 40.68 | 244.08 | | 244.08 |
| 21/05/2016 | | Chq no 654255 | Customer Receipt | | | -2,144.40 | 0.00 | 0.00 |
| | | | | | | 2,266.99 | | 2,266.99 |

## TASK 12

### Customer Activity Report (continued)

Hair Studio (122)

| Date | Number | Reference | Type | Net | VAT | Total | Discount | Outstanding |
|---|---|---|---|---|---|---|---|---|
| 30/04/2016 | | Inv 3098 | Customer OB Invoice | 681.60 | 0.00 | 681.60 | | 0.00 |
| 18/05/2016 | | Inv 3357 | Sales QE Invoice | 316.80 | 63.36 | 380.16 | | 380.16 |
| 18/05/2016 | | Inv 3357 | Sales QE Invoice | 881.92 | 176.38 | 1,058.30 | | 1,058.30 |
| 18/05/2016 | | Inv 3357 | Sales QE Invoice | 230.40 | 46.08 | 276.48 | | 276.48 |
| 21/05/2016 | | Chq no 452221 | Customer Receipt | | | -681.60 | 0.00 | 0.00 |
| | | | | | | 1,714.94 | | 1,714.94 |

Who: Leanne Halsall                     Produced by Sage One                     Page 1 of 2

| From: 30/04/2016 | Crazy Hair | 24 Apr 2017 |
|---|---|---|
| To:   31/05/2016 | **Customer Activity Report** | 13:38 |

Ribbons & Curls (138)

| Date | Number | Reference | Type | Net | VAT | Total | Discount | Outstanding |
|---|---|---|---|---|---|---|---|---|
| 30/04/2016 | | Inv 3123 | Customer OB Invoice | 391.20 | 0.00 | 391.20 | | 391.20 |
| 12/05/2016 | | Inv 3353 | Sales QE Invoice | 141.00 | 28.20 | 169.20 | | 169.20 |
| | | | | | | 560.40 | | 560.40 |

## TASK 12

### Supplier Activity Report

From: 30/04/2016
To: 31/05/2016

Crazy Hair
**Supplier Activity Report**

24 Apr 2017
13:40

#### Avada Cash & Carry (1134)

| Date | Number | Reference | Type | Net | VAT | Total | Discount | Outstanding |
|---|---|---|---|---|---|---|---|---|
| 30/04/2016 | | Inv C/251 | Supplier OB Invoice | 4,454.40 | 0.00 | 4,454.40 | | 0.00 |
| 11/05/2016 | | Inv C/910 | Purchase QE Invoice | 954.00 | 190.80 | 1,144.80 | | 1,144.80 |
| 31/05/2016 | | Chq No 163456 | Supplier Payment | | | -4,454.40 | 0.00 | 0.00 |
| | | | | | | 1,144.80 | | 1,144.80 |

#### Straightside Supplies (1138)

| Date | Number | Reference | Type | Net | VAT | Total | Discount | Outstanding |
|---|---|---|---|---|---|---|---|---|
| 30/04/2016 | | Inv 9140 | Supplier OB Invoice | 1,839.60 | 0.00 | 1,839.60 | | 1,839.60 |
| 11/05/2016 | | Inv 3362 | Purchase QE Invoice | 191.60 | 38.32 | 229.92 | | 229.92 |
| | | | | | | 2,069.52 | | 2,069.52 |

#### Hair Supplies (1165)

| Date | Number | Reference | Type | Net | VAT | Total | Discount | Outstanding |
|---|---|---|---|---|---|---|---|---|
| 30/04/2016 | | Inv 0028 | Supplier OB Invoice | 818.40 | 0.00 | 818.40 | | 0.00 |
| 13/05/2016 | | Inv 0814 | Purchase QE Invoice | 178.56 | 0.00 | 178.56 | | 178.56 |
| 31/05/2016 | | Chq no 163457 | Supplier Payment | | | -818.40 | 0.00 | 0.00 |
| | | | | | | 178.56 | | 178.56 |

#### Wigs Specialist (1185)

| Date | Number | Reference | Type | Net | VAT | Total | Discount | Outstanding |
|---|---|---|---|---|---|---|---|---|
| 30/04/2016 | | Inv S653 | Supplier OB Invoice | 102.00 | 0.00 | 102.00 | | 0.00 |
| 14/05/2016 | | Inv S1198 | Purchase QE Invoice | 3,393.60 | 678.72 | 4,072.32 | | 4,072.32 |
| 18/05/2016 | | C3223 | Purchase QE Credit | -102.70 | -20.54 | -123.24 | | -123.24 |
| 31/05/2016 | | Chq no 163455 | Supplier Payment | | | -102.00 | 0.00 | 0.00 |
| | | | | | | 3,949.08 | | 3,949.08 |

## TASK 12

### Aged Creditors Report (summary)

| To: 31/05/2016 | Crazy Hair | | | 24 Apr 2017 | | |
| --- | --- | --- | --- | --- | --- | --- |
| | **Aged Creditors Report** | | | 13:42 | | |
| Supplier | Credit limit | O/S Amt | < 30 days | < 60 days | < 90 days | Older |
| Aveda Cash & Carry (1134) | £5,500.00 | £1,144.80 | £1,144.80 | £0.00 | £0.00 | £0.00 |
| Hair Supplies (1165) | £4,000.00 | £178.56 | £178.56 | £0.00 | £0.00 | £0.00 |
| Straightside Supplies (1138) | £12,000.00 | £2,069.52 | £229.92 | £1,839.60 | £0.00 | £0.00 |
| Wigs Specialist (1185) | £5,000.00 | £3,949.08 | £3,949.08 | £0.00 | £0.00 | £0.00 |
| | TOTAL | £7,341.96 | £5,502.36 | £1,839.60 | £0.00 | £0.00 |

## TASK 12

### Aged Debtors Report (summary)

| To: 31/05/2016 | Crazy Hair | | | 24 Apr 2017 | | |
| --- | --- | --- | --- | --- | --- | --- |
| | **Aged Debtors Report** | | | 13:43 | | |
| Customer | Credit limit | O/S Amt | < 30 days | < 60 days | < 90 days | Older |
| Alfred Images (104) | £8,000.00 | £630.00 | £630.00 | £0.00 | £0.00 | £0.00 |
| Blades (118) | £6,100.00 | £2,266.99 | £2,266.99 | £0.00 | £0.00 | £0.00 |
| Figgaro (110) | £6,500.00 | £792.00 | £792.00 | £0.00 | £0.00 | £0.00 |
| Hair Studio (122) | £5,000.00 | £1,714.94 | £1,714.94 | £0.00 | £0.00 | £0.00 |
| Ribbons & Curls (138) | £5,000.00 | £560.40 | £169.20 | £391.20 | £0.00 | £0.00 |
| | TOTAL | £5,964.33 | £5,573.13 | £391.20 | £0.00 | £0.00 |

## Task 14

### Customer change of address

**Ribbons & Curls** (Customer)

Ref: 138

| OUTSTANDING [2] | OVERDUE [2] | SALES TO DATE [2] | SALES THIS YEAR [0] |
| --- | --- | --- | --- |
| £560.40 | £560.40 | £560.40 | £0.00 |
| CREDIT LIMIT | CREDIT TERMS | LAST SALE | AVERAGE SALE |
| £5,000.00 | 30 Days | 12 May 2016 | £280.20 |

Activity | Contacts and Addresses | Payment Details | Options | Notes

**Invoice Address** [MAIN]
Sales

122 Devonshire Road
Cranbrook
London
SE1 2AB
United Kingdom (GB)

**Main Contact** [MAIN]

## TASK 17

### Customer Address List

Crazy Hair
**Customer Address List**

25 Apr 2017
09:42

Address Types: All

| Customer Name | Address | Contact name | Phone | Mobile | Email | Fax |
|---|---|---|---|---|---|---|
| Alfred Images (104) | Masuki Offices<br>PO Box 5684<br>Birmingham<br>B23 4RD | Main Contact | | | | |
| Figgaro (110) | Beta Studio<br>34 Knightsbridge Way<br>Morden<br>SE23 4KA | Main Contact | | | | |
| Blades (118) | Alpha Studio<br>45 Key West<br>London<br>SE1 0JF | Main Contact | | | | |
| Hair Studio (122) | Framlington Court<br>Lee<br>London<br>SE4 7YH | Main Contact | | | | |
| Ribbons & Curls (138) | 122 Devonshire Road<br>Cranbrook<br>London<br>SE1 2AB | Main Contact | | | | |

## TASK 17

## Customer Activity

From: 30/04/2016
To: 31/05/2016

Crazy Hair
**Customer Activity Report**

25 Apr 2017
09:47

### Alfred Images (104)

| Date | Number | Reference | Type | Net | VAT | Total | Discount | Outstanding |
|---|---|---|---|---|---|---|---|---|
| 30/04/2016 | | Inv 3352 | Customer OB Invoice | 1,809.60 | 0.00 | 1,809.60 | | 0.00 |
| 12/05/2016 | | Inv 3354 | Sales QE Invoice | 581.00 | 116.20 | 697.20 | | 697.20 |
| 20/05/2016 | | Cheque no 183001 | Customer Receipt | | | -1,809.60 | 0.00 | 0.00 |
| 25/05/2016 | | CN23 | Sales QE Credit | -56.00 | -11.20 | -67.20 | | -67.20 |
| | | | | | | 630.00 | | 630.00 |

### Figgaro (110)

| Date | Number | Reference | Type | Net | VAT | Total | Discount | Outstanding |
|---|---|---|---|---|---|---|---|---|
| 30/04/2016 | | Inv 2856 | Customer OB Invoice | 3,880.80 | 0.00 | 3,880.80 | | 0.00 |
| 13/05/2016 | | Inv 3355 | Sales QE Invoice | 660.00 | 132.00 | 792.00 | | 792.00 |
| 21/05/2016 | | BACS | Customer Receipt | | | -3,880.80 | 0.00 | 0.00 |
| | | | | | | 792.00 | | 792.00 |

### Blades (118)

| Date | Number | Reference | Type | Net | VAT | Total | Discount | Outstanding |
|---|---|---|---|---|---|---|---|---|
| 30/04/2016 | | Inv 3345 | Customer OB Invoice | 2,144.40 | 0.00 | 2,144.40 | | 0.00 |
| 15/05/2016 | | Inv 3356 | Sales QE Invoice | 1,685.76 | 337.15 | 2,022.91 | | 2,022.91 |
| 15/05/2016 | | Inv 3356 | Sales QE Invoice | 203.40 | 40.68 | 244.08 | | 244.08 |
| 21/05/2016 | | Chq no 654255 | Customer Receipt | | | -2,144.40 | 0.00 | 0.00 |
| | | | | | | 2,266.99 | | 2,266.99 |

### Hair Studio (122)

| Date | Number | Reference | Type | Net | VAT | Total | Discount | Outstanding |
|---|---|---|---|---|---|---|---|---|
| 30/04/2016 | | Inv 3098 | Customer OB Invoice | 681.60 | 0.00 | 681.60 | | 0.00 |
| 18/05/2016 | | Inv 3357 | Sales QE Invoice | 316.80 | 63.36 | 380.16 | | 380.16 |
| 18/05/2016 | | Inv 3357 | Sales QE Invoice | 881.92 | 176.38 | 1,058.30 | | 1,058.30 |
| 18/05/2016 | | Inv 3357 | Sales QE Invoice | 230.40 | 46.08 | 276.48 | | 276.48 |
| 21/05/2016 | | Chq no 452221 | Customer Receipt | | | -681.60 | 0.00 | 0.00 |
| | | | | | | 1,714.94 | | 1,714.94 |

From: 30/04/2016
To: 31/05/2016

Crazy Hair
**Customer Activity Report**

25 Apr 2017
09:47

### Ribbons & Curls (138)

| Date | Number | Reference | Type | Net | VAT | Total | Discount | Outstanding |
|---|---|---|---|---|---|---|---|---|
| 30/04/2016 | | Inv 3123 | Customer OB Invoice | 391.20 | 0.00 | 391.20 | | 391.20 |
| 12/05/2016 | | Inv 3353 | Sales QE Invoice | 141.00 | 28.20 | 169.20 | | 169.20 |
| | | | | | | 560.40 | | 560.40 |

## TASK 17

### Supplier Activity

| From: 30/04/2016 | | Crazy Hair | | | 25 Apr 2017 |
|---|---|---|---|---|---|
| To: 31/05/2016 | | **Supplier Activity Report** | | | 09:49 |

**Avada Cash & Carry (1134)**

| Date | Number | Reference | Type | Net | VAT | Total | Discount | Outstanding |
|---|---|---|---|---|---|---|---|---|
| 30/04/2016 | | Inv C/251 | Supplier OB Invoice | 4,454.40 | 0.00 | 4,454.40 | | 0.00 |
| 11/05/2016 | | Inv C/910 | Purchase QE Invoice | 954.00 | 190.80 | 1,144.80 | | 1,144.80 |
| 31/05/2016 | | Chq No 163456 | Supplier Payment | | | -4,454.40 | 0.00 | 0.00 |
| | | | | | | 1,144.80 | | 1,144.80 |

**Straightside Supplies (1138)**

| Date | Number | Reference | Type | Net | VAT | Total | Discount | Outstanding |
|---|---|---|---|---|---|---|---|---|
| 30/04/2016 | | Inv 9140 | Supplier OB Invoice | 1,839.60 | 0.00 | 1,839.60 | | 1,839.60 |
| 11/05/2016 | | Inv 3362 | Purchase QE Invoice | 191.60 | 38.32 | 229.92 | | 229.92 |
| | | | | | | 2,069.52 | | 2,069.52 |

**Hair Supplies (1165)**

| Date | Number | Reference | Type | Net | VAT | Total | Discount | Outstanding |
|---|---|---|---|---|---|---|---|---|
| 30/04/2016 | | Inv 0028 | Supplier OB Invoice | 818.40 | 0.00 | 818.40 | | 0.00 |
| 13/05/2016 | | Inv 0814 | Purchase QE Invoice | 178.56 | 0.00 | 178.56 | | 178.56 |
| 31/05/2016 | | Chq no 163457 | Supplier Payment | | | -818.40 | 0.00 | 0.00 |
| | | | | | | 178.56 | | 178.56 |

**Wigs Specialist (1185)**

| Date | Number | Reference | Type | Net | VAT | Total | Discount | Outstanding |
|---|---|---|---|---|---|---|---|---|
| 30/04/2016 | | Inv S653 | Supplier OB Invoice | 102.00 | 0.00 | 102.00 | | 0.00 |
| 14/05/2016 | | Inv S1198 | Purchase QE Invoice | 3,393.60 | 678.72 | 4,072.32 | | 4,072.32 |
| 18/05/2016 | | C3223 | Purchase QE Credit | -102.70 | -20.54 | -123.24 | | -123.24 |
| 31/05/2016 | | Chq no 163455 | Supplier Payment | | | -102.00 | 0.00 | 0.00 |
| | | | | | | 3,949.08 | | 3,949.08 |

## TASK 17

### Trial Balance for the month of May

From: 30/04/2016
To: 31/05/2016

Crazy Hair
**Trial Balance Report**

25 Apr 2017
09:53

This period only

| Nominal Code | Name | Selected Period | |
|---|---|---|---|
| | | Debit | Credit |
| 0040 | Fixtures and fittings - Cost | 31,000.00 | |
| 0050 | Motor Vehicles - Cost | 24,000.00 | |
| 1100 | Trade Debtors | 5,964.33 | |
| 1200 | Current | 56,640.84 | |
| 1210 | Petty Cash | 185.69 | |
| 2100 | Trade Creditors | | 7,341.96 |
| 2200 | VAT on Sales | | 6,482.35 |
| 2201 | VAT on Purchases | 2,401.96 | |
| 3200 | Capital introduced | | 165,000.00 |
| 3260 | Drawings - equity | 5,440.00 | |
| 4000 | Sales - Brushes | | 1,204.30 |
| 4001 | Sales - Combs | | 187.00 |
| 4002 | Sales - Colours | | 4,172.85 |
| 4003 | Sales - Hairdryers | | 1,621.40 |
| 4004 | Sales - Wigs | | 8,167.68 |
| 4005 | Cash Sales | | 617.50 |
| 5000 | Purchases - Brushes | 1,064.60 | |
| 5001 | Purchases - Combs | 50.00 | |
| 5002 | Purchases - Colour | 5,154.00 | |
| 5003 | Purchases - Hairdryers | 6,488.56 | |
| 5004 | Purchases - Wigs | 56,104.90 | |
| 7200 | Electricity | 66.94 | |
| 7400 | Travel and Entertainment | 33.60 | |
| 7500 | Office costs | 4.51 | |
| 7610 | Premises Insurance | 168.00 | |
| 7900 | Bank charges and interest | 27.11 | |
| | TOTAL | £194,795.04 | £194,795.04 |

## TASK 17

## Audit Trail for May only (Detailed & include opening balance)

From: 30/04/2016
To: 31/05/2016

Crazy Hair
**Audit Trail Breakdown**

25 Apr 2017
09:55

Type: All, Status: All

| Trx No | Entry Date | User | Trx Date | Name | Type | Invoice Number | Ref | Ledger Account | Debit | Credit | Bank Reconciled |
|---|---|---|---|---|---|---|---|---|---|---|---|
| 1 | 21/04/2017 | LH | 30/04/2016 | Alfred Images (104) | Customer OB Invoice | | Inv 3352 | Opening Balances Control Account (9998) | | 1,809.60 | No |
| | | | | | | | | Trade Debtors (1100) | 1,809.60 | | No |
| 2 | 21/04/2017 | LH | 30/04/2016 | Figgaro (110) | Customer OB Invoice | | Inv 2856 | Opening Balances Control Account (9998) | | 3,860.80 | No |
| | | | | | | | | Trade Debtors (1100) | 3,860.80 | | No |
| 3 | 21/04/2017 | LH | 30/04/2016 | Blades (118) | Customer OB Invoice | | Inv 3345 | Opening Balances Control Account (9998) | | 2,144.40 | No |
| | | | | | | | | Trade Debtors (1100) | 2,144.40 | | No |
| 4 | 21/04/2017 | LH | 30/04/2016 | Hair Studio (122) | Customer OB Invoice | | Inv 3098 | Opening Balances Control Account (9998) | | 681.60 | No |
| | | | | | | | | Trade Debtors (1100) | 681.60 | | No |
| 5 | 21/04/2017 | LH | 30/04/2016 | Ribbons & Curls (138) | Customer OB Invoice | | Inv 3123 | Opening Balances Control Account (9998) | | 391.20 | No |
| | | | | | | | | Trade Debtors (1100) | 391.20 | | No |
| 6 | 21/04/2017 | LH | 30/04/2016 | Avada Cash & Carry (1134) | Supplier OB Invoice | | Inv C/251 | Trade Creditors (2100) | | 4,454.40 | No |
| | | | | | | | | Opening Balances Control Account (9998) | 4,454.40 | | No |
| 7 | 21/04/2017 | LH | 30/04/2016 | Straightside Supplies (1136) | Supplier OB Invoice | | Inv 9140 | Trade Creditors (2100) | | 1,839.60 | No |
| | | | | | | | | Opening Balances Control Account (9998) | 1,839.60 | | No |
| 8 | 21/04/2017 | LH | 30/04/2016 | Hair Supplies (1165) | Supplier OB Invoice | | Inv 0028 | Trade Creditors (2100) | | 818.40 | No |
| | | | | | | | | Opening Balances Control Account (9998) | 818.40 | | No |
| 9 | 21/04/2017 | LH | 30/04/2016 | Wig Specialists (1185) | Supplier OB Invoice | | Inv S653 | Trade Creditors (2100) | | 102.00 | No |
| | | | | | | | | Opening Balances Control Account (9998) | 102.00 | | No |
| 10 | 21/04/2017 | LH | 30/04/2016 | | Bank Opening Balance | | | Opening Balances Control Account (9998) | | 54,210.81 | No |
| | | | | | | | | Current (1200) | 54,210.81 | | Yes |
| 11 | 21/04/2017 | LH | 30/04/2016 | | Bank Opening Balance | | | Opening Balances Control Account (9998) | | 200.00 | No |
| | | | | | | | | Petty Cash (1210) | 200.00 | | No |

From: 30/04/2016
To: 31/05/2016

Crazy Hair
**Audit Trail Breakdown**

25 Apr 2017
09:55

| Trx No | Entry Date | User | Trx Date | Name | Type | Invoice Number | Ref | Ledger Account | Debit | Credit | Bank Reconciled |
|---|---|---|---|---|---|---|---|---|---|---|---|
| 12 | 21/04/2017 | LH | 30/04/2016 | | Journal Opening Balance | | OB 1/5/16 | Motor Vehicles - Cost (0050) | 24,000.00 | | No |
| | | | | | | | | Opening Balances Control Account (9998) | | 24,000.00 | No |
| | | | | | | | | Fixtures and fittings - Cost (0040) | 31,000.00 | | No |
| | | | | | | | | Opening Balances Control Account (9998) | | 31,000.00 | No |
| | | | | | | | | VAT on Sales (2200) | | 5,550.00 | No |
| | | | | | | | | Opening Balances Control Account (9998) | 5,550.00 | | No |
| | | | | | | | | VAT on Purchases (2201) | 1,507.94 | | No |
| | | | | | | | | Opening Balances Control Account (9998) | | 1,507.94 | No |
| | | | | | | | | Capital introduced (3200) | | 165,000.00 | No |
| | | | | | | | | Opening Balances Control Account (9998) | 165,000.00 | | No |
| | | | | | | | | Drawings - equity (3260) | 5,000.00 | | No |
| | | | | | | | | Opening Balances Control Account (9998) | | 5,000.00 | No |
| | | | | | | | | Sales - Brushes (4000) | | 345.00 | No |
| | | | | | | | | Opening Balances Control Account (9998) | 345.00 | | No |
| | | | | | | | | Sales - Combs (4001) | | 187.00 | No |
| | | | | | | | | Opening Balances Control Account (9998) | 187.00 | | No |
| | | | | | | | | Sales - Colours (4002) | | 3,801.45 | No |
| | | | | | | | | Opening Balances Control Account (9998) | 3,801.45 | | No |
| | | | | | | | | Sales - Hairdryers (4003) | | 758.00 | No |
| | | | | | | | | Opening Balances Control Account (9998) | 758.00 | | No |
| | | | | | | | | Sales - Wigs (4004) | | 5,600.00 | No |
| | | | | | | | | Opening Balances Control Account (9998) | 5,600.00 | | No |
| | | | | | | | | Cash Sales (4005) | | 617.50 | No |
| | | | | | | | | Opening Balances Control Account (9998) | 617.50 | | No |
| | | | | | | | | Purchases - Brushes (5000) | 873.00 | | No |
| | | | | | | | | Opening Balances Control Account (9998) | | 873.00 | No |

| From: 30/04/2016 | | | | | | | Crazy Hair | | | 25 Apr 2017 |
|---|---|---|---|---|---|---|---|---|---|---|
| To: 31/05/2016 | | | | | | | Audit Trail Breakdown | | | 09:55 |

| | | | | | | | | | | |
|---|---|---|---|---|---|---|---|---|---|---|
| | | | | | | | Purchases - Combs (5001) | 50.00 | | No |
| | | | | | | | Opening Balances Control Account (9998) | | 50.00 | No |
| | | | | | | | Purchases - Colour (5002) | 4,200.00 | | No |
| | | | | | | | Opening Balances Control Account (9998) | | 4,200.00 | No |
| | | | | | | | Purchases - Hairdryers (5003) | 6,310.00 | | No |
| | | | | | | | Opening Balances Control Account (9998) | | 6,310.00 | No |
| | | | | | | | Purchases - Wigs (5004) | 52,814.00 | | No |
| | | | | | | | Opening Balances Control Account (9998) | | 52,814.00 | No |
| 13 | 21/04/2017 | LH | 12/05/2016 | Ribbons & Curls (138) | Sales QE Invoice | Inv 3353 | Sales - Colours (4002) | | 141.00 | No |
| | | | | | | | VAT on Sales (2200) | | 28.20 | No |
| | | | | | | | Trade Debtors (1100) | 169.20 | | No |
| 14 | 21/04/2017 | LH | 12/05/2016 | Alfred Images (104) | Sales QE Invoice | Inv 3354 | Sales - Brushes (4000) | | 581.00 | No |
| | | | | | | | VAT on Sales (2200) | | 116.20 | No |
| | | | | | | | Trade Debtors (1100) | 697.20 | | No |
| 15 | 21/04/2017 | LH | 13/05/2016 | Figgaro (110) | Sales QE Invoice | Inv 3355 | Sales - Hairdryers (4003) | | 660.00 | No |
| | | | | | | | VAT on Sales (2200) | | 132.00 | No |
| | | | | | | | Trade Debtors (1100) | 792.00 | | No |
| 16 | 21/04/2017 | LH | 15/05/2016 | Blades (118) | Sales QE Invoice | Inv 3356 | Sales - Wigs (4004) | | 1,685.76 | No |
| | | | | | | | VAT on Sales (2200) | | 337.15 | No |
| | | | | | | | Trade Debtors (1100) | 2,022.91 | | No |
| 17 | 21/04/2017 | LH | 15/05/2016 | Blades (118) | Sales QE Invoice | Inv 3356 | Sales - Hairdryers (4003) | | 203.40 | No |
| | | | | | | | VAT on Sales (2200) | | 40.68 | No |
| | | | | | | | Trade Debtors (1100) | 244.08 | | No |
| 18 | 21/04/2017 | LH | 18/05/2016 | Hair Studio (122) | Sales QE Invoice | Inv 3357 | Sales - Brushes (4000) | | 316.80 | No |
| | | | | | | | VAT on Sales (2200) | | 63.36 | No |
| | | | | | | | Trade Debtors (1100) | 380.16 | | No |
| 19 | 21/04/2017 | LH | 18/05/2016 | Hair Studio (122) | Sales QE Invoice | Inv 3357 | Sales - Wigs (4004) | | 881.92 | No |
| | | | | | | | VAT on Sales (2200) | | 176.38 | No |
| | | | | | | | Trade Debtors (1100) | 1,058.30 | | No |
| 20 | 21/04/2017 | LH | 18/05/2016 | Hair Studio (122) | Sales QE Invoice | Inv 3357 | Sales - Colours (4002) | | 230.40 | No |
| | | | | | | | VAT on Sales (2200) | | 46.08 | No |
| | | | | | | | Trade Debtors (1100) | 276.48 | | No |
| 21 | 21/04/2017 | LH | 25/05/2016 | Alfred Images (104) | Sales QE Credit | CN23 | Trade Debtors (1100) | | 67.20 | No |
| | | | | | | | Sales - Brushes (4000) | 56.00 | | No |
| | | | | | | | VAT on Sales (2200) | 11.20 | | No |
| 22 | 21/04/2017 | LH | 11/05/2016 | Straightside Supplies (1138) | Purchase QE Invoice | Inv 3382 | Trade Creditors (2100) | | 229.92 | No |
| | | | | | | | Purchases - Brushes (5000) | 191.60 | | No |
| | | | | | | | VAT on Purchases (2201) | 38.32 | | No |
| 24 | 21/04/2017 | LH | 13/05/2016 | Hair Supplies (1165) | Purchase QE Invoice | Inv 0814 | Trade Creditors (2100) | | 178.56 | No |
| | | | | | | | Purchases - Hairdryers (5003) | 178.56 | | No |
| 25 | 21/04/2017 | LH | 14/05/2016 | Wig Specialists (1185) | Purchase QE Invoice | Inv S1198 | Trade Creditors (2100) | | 4,072.32 | No |
| | | | | | | | Purchases - Wigs (5004) | 3,393.60 | | No |
| | | | | | | | VAT on Purchases (2201) | 678.72 | | No |
| 26 | 21/04/2017 | LH | 18/05/2016 | Wig Specialists (1185) | Purchase QE Credit | C3223 | Purchases - Wigs (5004) | | 102.70 | No |
| | | | | | | | VAT on Purchases (2201) | | 20.54 | No |
| | | | | | | | Trade Creditors (2100) | 123.24 | | No |
| 27 | 24/04/2017 | LH | 20/05/2016 | Alfred Images (104) | Customer Receipt | Cheque no 183001 | Trade Debtors (1100) | | 1,809.60 | No |

| From: 30/04/2016<br>To: 31/05/2016 | | | | | Crazy Hair<br>**Audit Trail Breakdown** | | | | | 25 Apr 2017<br>09:55 |
|---|---|---|---|---|---|---|---|---|---|---|
| | | | | | | | Current (1200) | 1,809.60 | | Yes |
| 28 | 24/04/2017 | LH | 21/05/2016 | Blades (118) | Customer Receipt | Chq no 654255 | Trade Debtors (1100) | | 2,144.40 | No |
| | | | | | | | Current (1200) | 2,144.40 | | Yes |
| 29 | 24/04/2017 | LH | 21/05/2016 | Figgaro (110) | Customer Receipt | BACS | Trade Debtors (1100) | | 3,880.80 | No |
| | | | | | | | Current (1200) | 3,880.80 | | Yes |
| 30 | 24/04/2017 | LH | 21/05/2016 | Hair Studio (122) | Customer Receipt | Chq no 452221 | Trade Debtors (1100) | | 681.60 | No |
| | | | | | | | Current (1200) | 681.60 | | Yes |
| 31 | 24/04/2017 | LH | 31/05/2016 | Wigs Specialist (1185) | Supplier Payment | Chq no 163455 | Trade Creditors (2100) | 102.00 | | No |
| | | | | | | | Current (1200) | | 102.00 | No |
| 32 | 24/04/2017 | LH | 31/05/2016 | Avada Cash & Carry (1134) | Supplier Payment | Chq No 163456 | Trade Creditors (2100) | 4,454.40 | | No |
| | | | | | | | Current (1200) | | 4,454.40 | No |
| 33 | 24/04/2017 | LH | 31/05/2016 | Hair Supplies (1165) | Supplier Payment | Chq no 163457 | Trade Creditors (2100) | 818.40 | | No |
| | | | | | | | Current (1200) | | 818.40 | No |
| 34 | 24/04/2017 | LH | 19/05/2016 | | Other Payment | CSH 86 | Petty Cash (1210) | | 40.32 | No |
| | | | | | | | Travel and Entertainment (7400) | 33.60 | | No |
| | | | | | | | VAT on Purchases (2201) | 6.72 | | No |
| 35 | 24/04/2017 | LH | 20/05/2016 | | Other Payment | CSH 87 | Petty Cash (1210) | | 4.51 | No |
| | | | | | | | Office costs (7500) | 4.51 | | No |
| 36 | 24/04/2017 | LH | 20/05/2016 | | Other Receipt | 1001 | Sales - Brushes (4000) | | 17.50 | No |
| | | | | | | | VAT on Sales (2200) | | 3.50 | No |
| | | | | | | | Current (1200) | 21.00 | | Yes |
| 37 | 24/04/2017 | LH | 11/05/2016 | Avada Cash & Carry (1134) | Purchase QE Invoice | Inv C/910 | Trade Creditors (2100) | | 1,144.80 | No |
| | | | | | | | Purchases - Colour (5002) | 954.00 | | No |
| | | | | | | | VAT on Purchases (2201) | 190.80 | | No |
| 38 | 24/04/2017 | LH | 24/05/2016 | | Journal | JH12 | Drawings - equity (3260) | 440.00 | | No |
| | | | | | | | Current (1200) | | 440.00 | Yes |

| From: 30/04/2016<br>To: 31/05/2016 | | | | | Crazy Hair<br>**Audit Trail Breakdown** | | | | | 25 Apr 2017<br>09:55 |
|---|---|---|---|---|---|---|---|---|---|---|
| 39 | 24/04/2017 | LH | 31/05/2016 | | Bank Transfer | TRF01 | Current (1200) | | 30.52 | Yes |
| | | | | | | | Petty Cash (1210) | 30.52 | | No |
| 40 | 25/04/2017 | LH | 31/05/2016 | | Bank Payment | Bank Charge | Current (1200) | | 27.11 | Yes |
| | | | | | | | Bank charges and interest (7900) | 27.11 | | No |
| 41 | 25/04/2017 | LH | 24/05/2016 | | Other Payment | Coopers Union | Current (1200) | | 168.00 | Yes |
| | | | | | | | Premises Insurance (7610) | 168.00 | | No |
| 42 | 25/04/2017 | LH | 31/05/2016 | | Other Payment | Electricity | Current (1200) | | 66.94 | Yes |
| | | | | | | | Electricity (7200) | 66.94 | | No |

## TASK 17

### Aged Creditors (summary)

| | | | | | | |
|---|---|---|---|---|---|---|
| To: 31/05/2016 | | Crazy Hair **Aged Creditors Report** | | | 25 Apr 2017 09:57 | |
| Supplier | Credit limit | O/S Amt | < 30 days | < 60 days | < 90 days | Older |
| Avada Cash & Carry (1134) | £5,500.00 | £1,144.80 | £1,144.80 | £0.00 | £0.00 | £0.00 |
| Hair Supplies (1165) | £4,000.00 | £178.56 | £178.56 | £0.00 | £0.00 | £0.00 |
| Straightside Supplies (1138) | £12,000.00 | £2,069.52 | £229.92 | £1,839.60 | £0.00 | £0.00 |
| Wigs Specialist (1185) | £5,000.00 | £3,949.08 | £3,949.08 | £0.00 | £0.00 | £0.00 |
| | TOTAL | £7,341.96 | £5,502.36 | £1,839.60 | £0.00 | £0.00 |

## TASK 17

### Aged Debtors (summary)

| | | | | | | |
|---|---|---|---|---|---|---|
| To: 31/05/2016 | | Crazy Hair **Aged Debtors Report** | | | 25 Apr 2017 09:58 | |
| Customer | Credit limit | O/S Amt | < 30 days | < 60 days | < 90 days | Older |
| Alfred Images (104) | £8,000.00 | £630.00 | £630.00 | £0.00 | £0.00 | £0.00 |
| Blades (118) | £6,100.00 | £2,266.99 | £2,266.99 | £0.00 | £0.00 | £0.00 |
| Figgaro (110) | £6,500.00 | £792.00 | £792.00 | £0.00 | £0.00 | £0.00 |
| Hair Studio (122) | £5,000.00 | £1,714.94 | £1,714.94 | £0.00 | £0.00 | £0.00 |
| Ribbons & Curls (138) | £5,000.00 | £560.40 | £169.20 | £391.20 | £0.00 | £0.00 |
| | TOTAL | £5,964.33 | £5,573.13 | £391.20 | £0.00 | £0.00 |

## TASK 17

### Nominal Ledger Activity Report for Bank Current Account and Petty Cash Account

From: 30/04/2016
To:   31/05/2016

**Crazy Hair**
**Detailed Nominal Activity: Current (1200)**

25 Apr 2017
10:00

Transaction Type: All

| Trx No | Date | Invoice Number | Name | Type | Reference | Description | Debit | Credit | Running Total |
|---|---|---|---|---|---|---|---|---|---|
| | | | | | | Opening Balance | | 0.00 | |
| 10 | 30/04/2016 | | | Bank Opening Balance | | | | 54,210.81 | 54,210.81 Dr |
| 27 | 20/05/2016 | | Alfred Images (104) | Customer Receipt | Cheque no 183001 | | | 1,809.60 | 56,020.41 Dr |
| 36 | 20/05/2016 | | | Other Receipt | 1001 | | | 21.00 | 56,041.41 Dr |
| 28 | 21/05/2016 | | Blades (118) | Customer Receipt | Chq no 654255 | | | 2,144.40 | 58,185.81 Dr |
| 29 | 21/05/2016 | | Figgaro (110) | Customer Receipt | BACS | | | 3,880.80 | 62,066.61 Dr |
| 30 | 21/05/2016 | | Hair Studio (122) | Customer Receipt | Chq no 452221 | | | 681.60 | 62,748.21 Dr |
| 38 | 24/05/2016 | | | Journal | JH12 | | 440.00 | | 62,308.21 Dr |
| 41 | 24/05/2016 | | | Other Payment | Coopers Union | | 168.00 | | 62,140.21 Dr |
| 31 | 31/05/2016 | | Wigs Specialist (1185) | Supplier Payment | Chq no 163455 | | 102.00 | | 62,038.21 Dr |
| 32 | 31/05/2016 | | Avada Cash & Carry (1134) | Supplier Payment | Chq No 163456 | | 4,454.40 | | 57,583.81 Dr |
| 33 | 31/05/2016 | | Hair Supplies (1185) | Supplier Payment | Chq no 163457 | | 818.40 | | 56,765.41 Dr |
| 39 | 31/05/2016 | | | Bank Transfer | TRF01 | | 30.52 | | 56,734.89 Dr |
| 40 | 31/05/2016 | | | Bank Payment | Bank Charge | | 27.11 | | 56,707.78 Dr |
| 42 | 31/05/2016 | | | Other Payment | Electricity | | 66.94 | | 56,640.84 Dr |
| | | | | | | Closing Balance | 56,640.84 | | |
| | | | | | | Period Variance | 56,640.84 | | |

From: 30/04/2016
To:   31/05/2016

**Crazy Hair**
**Detailed Nominal Activity: Petty Cash (1210)**

25 Apr 2017
10:04

Transaction Type: All

| Trx No | Date | Invoice Number | Name | Type | Reference | Description | Debit | Credit | Running Total |
|---|---|---|---|---|---|---|---|---|---|
| | | | | | | Opening Balance | | 0.00 | |
| 11 | 30/04/2016 | | | Bank Opening Balance | | | | 200.00 | 200.00 Dr |
| 34 | 19/05/2016 | | | Other Payment | CSH 86 | | 40.32 | | 159.68 Dr |
| 35 | 20/05/2016 | | | Other Payment | CSH 87 | | 4.51 | | 155.17 Dr |
| 39 | 31/05/2016 | | | Bank Transfer | TRF01 | | | 30.52 | 185.69 Dr |
| | | | | | | Closing Balance | 185.69 | | |
| | | | | | | Period Variance | 185.69 | | |

# PRACTICE PAPER 3

## SHOES 4U ANSWERS

### TASK 3.3

**Customer Address List**

|  | Shoes 4U | | | | | | 25 Apr 2017 |
|  | **Customer Address List** | | | | | | 11:59 |

Address Types: All

| Customer Name | Address | Contact name | Phone | Mobile | Email | Fax |
|---|---|---|---|---|---|---|
| Beckers Gate Ltd (SL186) | Butchergate<br>Carlisle<br>Cumbria<br>C41 1SG | Main Contact | | | | |
| Eaton Bowls Club (SL213) | Seaton Street<br>St Neots<br>Cambs<br>PE19 8EF | Main Contact | | | | |
| Jones Footwear (SL302) | Scotby Village<br>Carlisle<br>Cumbria<br>C44 8BP | Main Contact | | | | |
| Dickens Ladies Footwear (SL307) | 17 Royal Square<br>Bleachfield<br>North Yorkshire<br>YO87 9AD | Main Contact | | | | |

### TASK 3.3

**Supplier Address List**

|  | Shoes 4U | | | | | | 25 Apr 2017 |
|  | **Supplier Address List** | | | | | | 12:01 |

Address Types: All

| Supplier Name | Address | Contact name | Phone | Mobile | Email | Fax |
|---|---|---|---|---|---|---|
| Bootsy & Smudge Ltd (PL112) | Factory Road<br>Stilton<br>Cambs<br>PE7 3RP | Main Contact | | | | |
| Briggsthorpe Boots (PL168) | Long Buckby Wharf<br>Long Buckby<br>Northampton<br>NN4 9UW | Main Contact | | | | |
| Gallows Fashion (PL172) | 18 The Crescent<br>Pickford<br>Cambs<br>PE7 8QV | Main Contact | | | | |
| Dickens Ladies Footwear (PL173) | 17 Royal Square<br>Bleachfield<br>North Yorkshire<br>YO87 9AD | Main Contact | | | | |

KAPLAN PUBLISHING

## TASK 3.3

### Trial Balance

From: 31/05/2016
To:   30/06/2016

Shoes 4U
**Trial Balance Report**

25 Apr 2017
12:03

This period only

| Nominal Code | Name | Selected Period | |
| --- | --- | --- | --- |
| | | Debit | Credit |
| 0030 | Freehold Property | 72,000.00 | |
| 0040 | Fixtures and fittings - Cost | 9,000.00 | |
| 0050 | Motor Vehicles - Cost | 7,500.00 | |
| 1100 | Trade Debtors | 10,386.27 | |
| 1200 | Current | 14,363.00 | |
| 1210 | Cash | 200.00 | |
| 1220 | Deposit | 5,000.00 | |
| 2100 | Trade Creditors | | 47,048.26 |
| 2200 | VAT on Sales | | 3,402.35 |
| 2201 | VAT on Purchases | 1,130.00 | |
| 3200 | Capital introduced | | 30,000.00 |
| 3260 | Drawings - equity | 600.00 | |
| 4000 | Sales - Men's Footwear | | 79,320.00 |
| 4001 | Sales - Ladies Footwear | | 43,210.00 |
| 4002 | Cash Sales | | 6,798.00 |
| 5000 | Purchases - Men's Footwear | 55,432.00 | |
| 5001 | Purchases - Ladies Footwear | 23,410.00 | |
| 6200 | Advertising | 7,231.00 | |
| 7100 | Rent | 1,263.00 | |
| 7200 | Electricity | 567.34 | |
| 7500 | Telephone | 866.00 | |
| 7501 | Office Stationery | 830.00 | |
| | TOTAL | £209,778.61 | £209,778.61 |

**TASK 7**

Remittance Advices

# Remittance Advice

Date Paid: 18/06/2016

Reference: PL172

| Gallows Fashion | Shoes 4U |
|---|---|
| 18 The Crescent | 85 Barrington Close |
| Pickford | Carlisle |
| Cambs | Cumbria |
| PE7 8QV | C41 3ED |
| | United Kingdom |

Telephone: 01234 567891

VAT Number: GB 123456789

**Reference:** Chq no 109887

| Our Ref | Your Ref | Date | Total Amount | Amount Paid |
|---|---|---|---|---|
| Inv G-01239 | | 31/05/2016 | 400.00 | 400.00 |
| | | | **Total Paid:** | **£ 400.00 GBP** |

# Remittance Advice

Date Paid: 18/06/2016

Reference: PL168

| Briggsthorpe Boots | Shoes 4U |
|---|---|
| Long Buckby Wharf | 85 Barrington Close |
| Long Buckby | Carlisle |
| Northampton | Cumbria |
| NN4 9UW | C41 3ED |
| | United Kingdom |

Telephone: 01234 567891

VAT Number: GB 123456789

**Reference:** Chq no 109888

| Our Ref | Your Ref | Date | Total Amount | Amount Paid |
|---|---|---|---|---|
| Inv 0001087 | | 31/05/2016 | 43,200.00 | 23,300.00 |
| | | | **Total Paid:** | **£ 23,300.00 GBP** |

## TASK 10

### Trial Balance

From: 31/05/2016
To:   30/06/2016

Shoes 4U
**Trial Balance Report**

25 Apr 2017
12:46

This period only

| Nominal Code | Name | Selected Period | |
|---|---|---|---|
| | | Debit | Credit |
| 0030 | Freehold Property | 72,000.00 | |
| 0040 | Fixtures and fittings - Cost | 9,000.00 | |
| 0050 | Motor Vehicles - Cost | 7,500.00 | |
| 1100 | Trade Debtors | 6,874.56 | |
| 1200 | Current | 319.80 | |
| 1210 | Cash | 200.00 | |
| 1220 | Deposit | 5,000.00 | |
| 2100 | Trade Creditors | | 29,948.26 |
| 2200 | VAT on Sales | | 4,430.43 |
| 2201 | VAT on Purchases | 2,232.25 | |
| 3200 | Capital introduced | | 30,000.00 |
| 3260 | Drawings - equity | 600.00 | |
| 4000 | Sales - Men's Footwear | | 81,669.66 |
| 4001 | Sales - Ladies Footwear | | 46,000.75 |
| 4002 | Cash Sales | | 6,798.00 |
| 5000 | Purchases - Men's Footwear | 60,432.00 | |
| 5001 | Purchases - Ladies Footwear | 23,910.00 | |
| 6200 | Advertising | 7,231.00 | |
| 7100 | Rent | 1,263.00 | |
| 7200 | Electricity | 567.34 | |
| 7500 | Telephone | 866.00 | |
| 7501 | Office Stationery | 841.25 | |
| 7502 | Refreshments | 9.90 | |
| | TOTAL | £198,847.10 | £198,847.10 |

## TASK 10

### Sales Day Book

| From: 31/05/2016 | | | | | | Shoes 4U | | | | | 25 Apr 2017 |
| To: 30/06/2016 | | | | | | **Sales Day Book Report** | | | | | 12:48 |

Type: Sales QE Invoice

| Trx No | Type | Date | Name | Invoice Number | Ref | Details | Net | VAT | Total |
|---|---|---|---|---|---|---|---|---|---|
| 13 | Sales QE Invoice | 04/06/2016 | Beckers Gate Ltd | | Inv 1622 | | 450.00 | 90.00 | 540.00 |
| 14 | Sales QE Invoice | 06/06/2016 | Eaton Bowls Club | | Inv 1623 | | 1,385.00 | 277.00 | 1,662.00 |
| 15 | Sales QE Invoice | 14/06/2016 | Dickens Ladies Footwear | | Inv 1624 | | 450.00 | 90.00 | 540.00 |
| 16 | Sales QE Invoice | 14/06/2016 | Dickens Ladies Footwear | | Inv 1624 | | 1,850.00 | 370.00 | 2,220.00 |
| 17 | Sales QE Invoice | 17/06/2016 | Jones Footwear | | Inv 1625 | | 1,175.75 | 235.15 | 1,410.90 |
| | | | | | | TOTAL | £5,310.75 | £1,062.15 | £6,372.90 |

## TASK 10

### Customer Activity Report

| From: 31/05/2016 | | | | | Shoes 4U | | | | 25 Apr 2017 |
| To: 30/06/2016 | | | | | **Customer Activity Report** | | | | 12:49 |

**Beckers Gate Ltd (SL186)**

| Date | Number | Reference | Type | Net | VAT | Total | Discount | Outstanding |
|---|---|---|---|---|---|---|---|---|
| 31/05/2016 | | Inv 1613 | Customer OB Invoice | 4,811.88 | 0.00 | 4,811.88 | | 0.00 |
| 04/06/2016 | | Inv 1622 | Sales QE Invoice | 450.00 | 90.00 | 540.00 | | 540.00 |
| 11/06/2016 | | Chq no 199846 | Customer Receipt | | | -4,811.88 | 0.00 | 0.00 |
| | | | | | | 540.00 | | 540.00 |

**Eaton Bowls Club (SL213)**

| Date | Number | Reference | Type | Net | VAT | Total | Discount | Outstanding |
|---|---|---|---|---|---|---|---|---|
| 31/05/2016 | | Inv 1582 | Customer OB Invoice | 961.98 | 0.00 | 961.98 | | 0.00 |
| 06/06/2016 | | Inv 1623 | Sales QE Invoice | 1,385.00 | 277.00 | 1,662.00 | | 1,662.00 |
| 14/06/2016 | | Chq No 107654 | Customer Receipt | | | -961.98 | 0.00 | 0.00 |
| | | | | | | 1,662.00 | | 1,662.00 |

**Jones Footwear (SL302)**

| Date | Number | Reference | Type | Net | VAT | Total | Discount | Outstanding |
|---|---|---|---|---|---|---|---|---|
| 31/05/2016 | | Inv 1596 | Customer OB Invoice | 3,828.75 | 0.00 | 3,828.75 | | 0.00 |
| 14/06/2016 | | 244536 | Customer Receipt | | | -3,828.75 | 0.00 | 0.00 |
| 17/06/2016 | | Inv 1625 | Sales QE Invoice | 1,175.75 | 235.15 | 1,410.90 | | 1,410.90 |
| | | | | | | 1,410.90 | | 1,410.90 |

**Dickens Ladies Footwear (SL307)**

| Date | Number | Reference | Type | Net | VAT | Total | Discount | Outstanding |
|---|---|---|---|---|---|---|---|---|
| 31/05/2016 | | Inv 1601 | Customer OB Invoice | 783.66 | 0.00 | 783.66 | | 783.66 |
| 08/06/2016 | | Credit note no CR10 | Sales QE Credit | -235.00 | -47.00 | -282.00 | | -282.00 |
| 14/06/2016 | | Inv 1624 | Sales QE Invoice | 450.00 | 90.00 | 540.00 | | 540.00 |
| 14/06/2016 | | Inv 1624 | Sales QE Invoice | 1,850.00 | 370.00 | 2,220.00 | | 2,220.00 |
| | | | | | | 3,261.66 | | 3,261.66 |

## TASK 10

### Supplier Activity Report

From: 31/05/2016
To:   30/06/2016

Shoes 4U
**Supplier Activity Report**

25 Apr 2017
12:50

#### Bootsy & Smudge Ltd (PL112)

| Date | Number | Reference | Type | Net | VAT | Total | Discount | Outstanding |
|---|---|---|---|---|---|---|---|---|
| 31/05/2016 | | Inv B/468 | Supplier OB Invoice | 2,881.26 | 0.00 | 2,881.26 | | 2,881.26 |
| 02/06/2016 | | Inv B/752 | Purchase QE Invoice | 300.00 | 60.00 | 360.00 | | 360.00 |
| 13/06/2016 | | inv B/753 | Purchase QE Invoice | 200.00 | 40.00 | 240.00 | | 240.00 |
| | | | | | | **3,481.26** | | **3,481.26** |

#### Briggsthorpe Boots (PL168)

| Date | Number | Reference | Type | Net | VAT | Total | Discount | Outstanding |
|---|---|---|---|---|---|---|---|---|
| 31/05/2016 | | Inv 0001087 | Supplier OB Invoice | 43,200.00 | 0.00 | 43,200.00 | | 19,900.00 |
| 10/06/2016 | | Inv 12350 | Purchase QE Invoice | 2,500.00 | 500.00 | 3,000.00 | | 3,000.00 |
| 18/06/2016 | | Chq no 109888 | Supplier Payment | | | -23,300.00 | 0.00 | 0.00 |
| | | | | | | **22,900.00** | | **22,900.00** |

#### Gallows Fashion (PL172)

| Date | Number | Reference | Type | Net | VAT | Total | Discount | Outstanding |
|---|---|---|---|---|---|---|---|---|
| 31/05/2016 | | Inv G-01239 | Supplier OB Invoice | 400.00 | 0.00 | 400.00 | | 0.00 |
| 12/06/2016 | | Inv G-2285 | Purchase QE Invoice | 2,500.00 | 500.00 | 3,000.00 | | 3,000.00 |
| 18/06/2016 | | Chq no 109887 | Supplier Payment | | | -400.00 | 0.00 | 0.00 |
| | | | | | | **3,000.00** | | **3,000.00** |

#### Dickens Ladies Footwear (PL173)

| Date | Number | Reference | Type | Net | VAT | Total | Discount | Outstanding |
|---|---|---|---|---|---|---|---|---|
| 31/05/2016 | | Inv 06345 | Supplier OB Invoice | 567.00 | 0.00 | 567.00 | | 567.00 |
| | | | | | | **567.00** | | **567.00** |

## TASK 10

## Aged Creditors Report (detailed)

| | | | | Shoes 4U | | | 25 Apr 2017 | |
|---|---|---|---|---|---|---|---|---|
| | | | **Aged Creditors Breakdown** | | | | 12:52 | |
| Date | Reference | Total | Due Date | O/S Amt | < 30 days | < 60 days | < 90 days | Older |
| **Bootsy & Smudge Ltd (PL112), Credit limit: £4,000.00** | | | | | | | | |
| **, Terms: 30 days - OVERDUE** | | | | | | | | |
| 31/05/2016 | Inv B/468 | 2,881.26 | 30/06/2016 | 2,881.26 | | 2,881.26 | | |
| 02/06/2016 | Inv B/752 | 360.00 | 02/07/2016 | 360.00 | 360.00 | | | |
| 13/06/2016 | inv B/753 | 240.00 | 13/07/2016 | 240.00 | 240.00 | | | |
| | | | | £3,481.26 | £600.00 | £2,881.26 | £0.00 | £0.00 |
| **Briggsthorpe Boots (PL168), Credit limit: £50,000.00** | | | | | | | | |
| **, Terms: 30 days - OVERDUE** | | | | | | | | |
| 31/05/2016 | Inv 0001087 | 43,200.00 | 30/06/2016 | 19,900.00 | | 19,900.00 | | |
| 10/06/2016 | Inv 12350 | 3,000.00 | 10/07/2016 | 3,000.00 | 3,000.00 | | | |
| | | | | £22,900.00 | £3,000.00 | £19,900.00 | £0.00 | £0.00 |
| **Dickens Ladies Footwear (PL173), Credit limit: £2,000.00** | | | | | | | | |
| **, Terms: 30 days - OVERDUE** | | | | | | | | |
| 31/05/2016 | Inv 06345 | 567.00 | 30/06/2016 | 567.00 | | 567.00 | | |
| | | | | £567.00 | £0.00 | £567.00 | £0.00 | £0.00 |
| **Gallows Fashion (PL172), Credit limit: £2,000.00** | | | | | | | | |
| **, Terms: 30 days - OVERDUE** | | | | | | | | |
| 12/06/2016 | Inv G-2285 | 3,000.00 | 12/07/2016 | 3,000.00 | 3,000.00 | | | |
| | | | | £3,000.00 | £3,000.00 | £0.00 | £0.00 | £0.00 |
| | | | **TOTAL** | £29,948.26 | £6,600.00 | £23,348.26 | £0.00 | £0.00 |

## TASK 10

### Aged Debtors Report (detailed)

| | Shoes 4U | | | | | | | 25 Apr 2017 |
| --- | --- | --- | --- | --- | --- | --- | --- | --- |
| To: 30/06/2016 | | | **Aged Debtors Breakdown** | | | | | 12:54 |

| Date | Reference | Total | Due Date | O/S Amt | < 30 days | < 60 days | < 90 days | Older |
| --- | --- | --- | --- | --- | --- | --- | --- | --- |
| Beckers Gate Ltd (SL186), Credit limit: £5,000.00 | | | | | | | | |
| , Terms: 30 days - OVERDUE | | | | | | | | |
| 04/06/2016 | QE-Inv 1622 | 540.00 | 04/07/2016 | 540.00 | 540.00 | | | |
| | | | | £540.00 | £540.00 | £0.00 | £0.00 | £0.00 |
| | | | | | | | | |
| Dickens Ladies Footwear (SL307), Credit limit: £11,000.00 | | | | | | | | |
| , Terms: 30 days - OVERDUE | | | | | | | | |
| 31/05/2016 | OB-Inv 1601 | 783.66 | 30/06/2016 | 783.66 | | 783.66 | | |
| 08/06/2016 | QE-Credit note no CR10 | -282.00 | | -282.00 | -282.00 | | | |
| 14/06/2016 | QE-Inv 1624 | 540.00 | 14/07/2016 | 540.00 | 540.00 | | | |
| 14/06/2016 | QE-Inv 1624 | 2,220.00 | 14/07/2016 | 2,220.00 | 2,220.00 | | | |
| | | | | £3,261.66 | £2,478.00 | £783.66 | £0.00 | £0.00 |
| | | | | | | | | |
| Eaton Bowls Club (SL213), Credit limit: £3,000.00 | | | | | | | | |
| , Terms: 30 days - OVERDUE | | | | | | | | |
| 06/06/2016 | QE-Inv 1623 | 1,662.00 | 06/07/2016 | 1,662.00 | 1,662.00 | | | |
| | | | | £1,662.00 | £1,662.00 | £0.00 | £0.00 | £0.00 |
| | | | | | | | | |
| Jones Footwear (SL302), Credit limit: £6,000.00 | | | | | | | | |
| , Terms: 30 days - OVERDUE | | | | | | | | |
| 17/06/2016 | QE-Inv 1625 | 1,410.90 | 17/07/2016 | 1,410.90 | 1,410.90 | | | |
| | | | | £1,410.90 | £1,410.90 | £0.00 | £0.00 | £0.00 |
| | | TOTAL | | £6,874.56 | £6,090.90 | £783.66 | £0.00 | £0.00 |

## TASK 10

## Nominal Ledger Activity Report for Bank Current Account and Petty Cash Account

Shoes 4U
**Detailed Nominal Activity: Current (1200)**

Transaction Type: All

| Trx No | Date | Invoice Number | Name | Type | Reference | Description | Debit | Credit | Running Total |
|---|---|---|---|---|---|---|---|---|---|
| | | | | | | Opening Balance | | 0.00 | |
| 9 | 31/05/2016 | | | Bank Opening Balance | | | 19,363.00 | | 19,363.00 Dr |
| 12 | 01/06/2016 | | | Bank Transfer | TRF01 | | | 5,000.00 | 14,363.00 Dr |
| 30 | 10/06/2016 | | | Bank Transfer | TRF02 | | | 23.40 | 14,339.60 Dr |
| 23 | 11/06/2016 | | Beckers Gate Ltd (SL186) | Customer Receipt | Chq no 199846 | | 4,811.88 | | 19,151.48 Dr |
| 24 | 14/06/2016 | | Eaton Bowls Club (SL213) | Customer Receipt | Chq No 107654 | | 961.98 | | 20,113.46 Dr |
| 25 | 14/06/2016 | | Jones Footwear (SL302) | Customer Receipt | 244536 | | 3,828.75 | | 23,942.21 Dr |
| 26 | 18/06/2016 | | Gallows Fashion (PL172) | Supplier Payment | Chq no 109887 | | | 400.00 | 23,542.21 Dr |
| 27 | 18/06/2016 | | Briggsthorpe Boots (PL168) | Supplier Payment | Chq no 109888 | | | 23,300.00 | 242.21 Dr |
| 31 | 23/06/2016 | | | Other Receipt | F027 | | 77.59 | | 319.80 Dr |
| | | | | | | Closing Balance | 319.80 | | |
| | | | | | | Period Variance | 319.80 | | |

Shoes 4U
**Detailed Nominal Activity: Cash (1210)**

Transaction Type: All

| Trx No | Date | Invoice Number | Name | Type | Reference | Description | Debit | Credit | Running Total |
|---|---|---|---|---|---|---|---|---|---|
| | | | | | | Opening Balance | | 0.00 | |
| 10 | 31/05/2016 | | | Bank Opening Balance | | | 200.00 | | 200.00 Dr |
| 28 | 05/06/2016 | | | Other Payment | Voucher no 010 | | | 9.90 | 190.10 Dr |
| 29 | 10/06/2016 | | | Other Payment | Voucher no 011 | | | 13.50 | 176.60 Dr |
| 30 | 10/06/2016 | | | Bank Transfer | TRF02 | | 23.40 | | 200.00 Dr |
| | | | | | | Closing Balance | 200.00 | | |
| | | | | | | Period Variance | 200.00 | | |

## TASK 11.1

Recurring payment

## Task 11.2

Recurring receipt

## TASK 15

## Trial Balance

| From: 31/05/2016 | Shoes 4U | 25 Apr 2017 |
| To:   30/06/2016 | **Trial Balance Report** | 14:16 |

This period only

| Nominal Code | Name | Selected Period | |
| --- | --- | --- | --- |
| | | Debit | Credit |
| 0030 | Freehold Property | 72,000.00 | |
| 0040 | Fixtures and fittings - Cost | 9,000.00 | |
| 0050 | Motor Vehicles - Cost | 7,500.00 | |
| 1100 | Trade Debtors | 6,874.56 | |
| 1200 | Current | | 1,569.20 |
| 1210 | Cash | 200.00 | |
| 1220 | Deposit | 5,000.00 | |
| 2100 | Trade Creditors | | 29,948.26 |
| 2200 | VAT on Sales | | 4,439.43 |
| 2201 | VAT on Purchases | 2,232.25 | |
| 3200 | Capital introduced | | 30,000.00 |
| 3260 | Drawings - equity | 3,800.00 | |
| 4000 | Sales - Men's Footwear | | 81,669.66 |
| 4001 | Sales - Ladies Footwear | | 46,045.75 |
| 4002 | Cash Sales | | 6,798.00 |
| 4900 | Other income | | 1,500.00 |
| 5000 | Purchases - Men's Footwear | 60,432.00 | |
| 5001 | Purchases - Ladies Footwear | 23,910.00 | |
| 6200 | Advertising | 7,231.00 | |
| 7100 | Rent | 1,263.00 | |
| 7200 | Electricity | 760.34 | |
| 7500 | Telephone | 866.00 | |
| 7501 | Office Stationery | 841.25 | |
| 7502 | Refreshments | 9.90 | |
| 7900 | Bank charges and interest | 50.00 | |
| | TOTAL | £201,970.30 | £201,970.30 |

# TASK 15

## Audit Trail

Shoes 4U
**Audit Trail Breakdown**

Type: All, Status: All

| Trx No | Entry Date | User | Trx Date | Name | Type | Invoice Number | Ref | Ledger Account | Debit | Credit | Bank Reconciled |
|---|---|---|---|---|---|---|---|---|---|---|---|
| 1 | 25/04/2017 | LH | 31/05/2016 | Beckers Gate Ltd (SL186) | Customer OB Invoice | | Inv 1613 | Opening Balances Control Account (9998) | | 4,811.88 | No |
| | | | | | | | | Trade Debtors (1100) | 4,811.88 | | No |
| 2 | 25/04/2017 | LH | 31/05/2016 | Eaton Bowls Club (SL213) | Customer OB Invoice | | Inv 1562 | Opening Balances Control Account (9998) | | 961.96 | No |
| | | | | | | | | Trade Debtors (1100) | 961.96 | | No |
| 3 | 25/04/2017 | LH | 31/05/2016 | Jones Footwear (SL302) | Customer OB Invoice | | Inv 1596 | Opening Balances Control Account (9998) | | 3,828.75 | No |
| | | | | | | | | Trade Debtors (1100) | 3,828.75 | | No |
| 4 | 25/04/2017 | LH | 31/05/2016 | Dickens Ladies Footwear (SL307) | Customer OB Invoice | | Inv 1601 | Opening Balances Control Account (9998) | | 783.66 | No |
| | | | | | | | | Trade Debtors (1100) | 783.66 | | No |
| 5 | 25/04/2017 | LH | 31/05/2016 | Bootsy & Smudge Ltd (PL112) | Supplier OB Invoice | | Inv B/468 | Trade Creditors (2100) | | 2,881.26 | No |
| | | | | | | | | Opening Balances Control Account (9998) | 2,881.26 | | No |
| 6 | 25/04/2017 | LH | 31/05/2016 | Briggsthorpe Boots (PL168) | Supplier OB Invoice | | Inv 0001087 | Trade Creditors (2100) | | 43,200.00 | No |
| | | | | | | | | Opening Balances Control Account (9998) | 43,200.00 | | No |
| 7 | 25/04/2017 | LH | 31/05/2016 | Gallows Fashion (PL172) | Supplier OB Invoice | | Inv G-01239 | Trade Creditors (2100) | | 400.00 | No |
| | | | | | | | | Opening Balances Control Account (9998) | 400.00 | | No |
| 8 | 25/04/2017 | LH | 31/05/2016 | Dickens Ladies Footwear (PL173) | Supplier OB Invoice | | Inv 06345 | Trade Creditors (2100) | | 567.00 | No |
| | | | | | | | | Opening Balances Control Account (9998) | 567.00 | | No |
| 9 | 25/04/2017 | LH | 31/05/2016 | | Bank Opening Balance | | | Opening Balances Control Account (9998) | | 19,363.00 | No |
| | | | | | | | | Current (1200) | 19,363.00 | | Yes |
| 10 | 25/04/2017 | LH | 31/05/2016 | | Bank Opening Balance | | | Opening Balances Control Account (9998) | | 200.00 | No |
| | | | | | | | | Cash (1210) | 200.00 | | No |
| 11 | 25/04/2017 | LH | 31/05/2016 | | Journal Opening Balance | | OB 1/6/16 | Freehold Property (0030) | 72,000.00 | | No |
| | | | | | | | | Opening Balances Control Account (9998) | | 72,000.00 | No |

Shoes 4U
**Audit Trail Breakdown**

| | | Debit | Credit | Bank Reconciled |
|---|---|---|---|---|
| | Motor Vehicles - Cost (0050) | 7,500.00 | | No |
| | Opening Balances Control Account (9998) | | 7,500.00 | No |
| | Fixtures and fittings - Cost (0040) | 9,000.00 | | No |
| | Opening Balances Control Account (9998) | | 9,000.00 | No |
| | VAT on Sales (2200) | | 3,402.35 | No |
| | Opening Balances Control Account (9998) | 3,402.35 | | No |
| | VAT on Purchases (2201) | 1,130.00 | | No |
| | Opening Balances Control Account (9998) | | 1,130.00 | No |
| | Capital introduced (3200) | | 30,000.00 | No |
| | Opening Balances Control Account (9998) | 30,000.00 | | No |
| | Drawings - equity (3260) | 600.00 | | No |
| | Opening Balances Control Account (9998) | | 600.00 | No |
| | Sales - Men's Footwear (4000) | | 79,320.00 | No |
| | Opening Balances Control Account (9998) | 79,320.00 | | No |
| | Sales - Ladies Footwear (4001) | | 43,210.00 | No |
| | Opening Balances Control Account (9998) | 43,210.00 | | No |
| | Cash Sales (4002) | | 6,798.00 | No |
| | Opening Balances Control Account (9998) | 6,798.00 | | No |
| | Purchases - Men's Footwear (5000) | 55,432.00 | | No |
| | Opening Balances Control Account (9998) | | 55,432.00 | No |
| | Purchases - Ladies Footwear (5001) | 23,410.00 | | No |
| | Opening Balances Control Account (9998) | | 23,410.00 | No |
| | Advertising (6200) | 7,231.00 | | No |
| | Opening Balances Control Account (9998) | | 7,231.00 | No |
| | Telephone (7500) | 866.00 | | No |
| | Opening Balances Control Account (9998) | | 866.00 | No |

From: 31/05/2016
To: 30/06/2016

Shoes 4U
Audit Trail Breakdown

25 Apr 2017
14:18

| | | | | | | | | | | |
|---|---|---|---|---|---|---|---|---|---|---|
| | | | | | | Rent (7100) | 1,263.00 | | No |
| | | | | | | Opening Balances Control Account (9998) | | 1,263.00 | No |
| | | | | | | Electricity (7200) | 567.34 | | No |
| | | | | | | Opening Balances Control Account (9998) | | 567.34 | No |
| | | | | | | Office Stationery (7501) | 830.00 | | No |
| | | | | | | Opening Balances Control Account (9998) | | 830.00 | No |
| 12 | 25/04/2017 | LH | 01/06/2016 | | Bank Transfer | TRF01 | Current (1200) | | 5,000.00 | Yes |
| | | | | | | | Deposit (1220) | 5,000.00 | | No |
| 13 | 25/04/2017 | LH | 04/06/2016 | Beckers Gate Ltd (SL166) | Sales QE Invoice | Inv 1622 | Sales - Men's Footwear (4000) | | 450.00 | No |
| | | | | | | | VAT on Sales (2200) | | 90.00 | No |
| | | | | | | | Trade Debtors (1100) | 540.00 | | No |
| 14 | 25/04/2017 | LH | 06/06/2016 | Eaton Bowls Club (SL213) | Sales QE Invoice | Inv 1623 | Sales - Men's Footwear (4000) | | 1,385.00 | No |
| | | | | | | | VAT on Sales (2200) | | 277.00 | No |
| | | | | | | | Trade Debtors (1100) | 1,662.00 | | No |
| 15 | 25/04/2017 | LH | 14/06/2016 | Dickens Ladies Footwear (SL307) | Sales QE Invoice | Inv 1624 | Sales - Men's Footwear (4000) | | 450.00 | No |
| | | | | | | | VAT on Sales (2200) | | 90.00 | No |
| | | | | | | | Trade Debtors (1100) | 540.00 | | No |
| 16 | 25/04/2017 | LH | 14/06/2016 | Dickens Ladies Footwear (SL307) | Sales QE Invoice | Inv 1624 | Sales - Ladies Footwear (4001) | | 1,850.00 | No |
| | | | | | | | VAT on Sales (2200) | | 370.00 | No |
| | | | | | | | Trade Debtors (1100) | 2,220.00 | | No |
| 17 | 25/04/2017 | LH | 17/06/2016 | Jones Footwear (SL302) | Sales QE Invoice | Inv 1625 | Sales - Ladies Footwear (4001) | | 1,175.75 | No |
| | | | | | | | VAT on Sales (2200) | | 235.15 | No |
| | | | | | | | Trade Debtors (1100) | 1,410.90 | | No |
| 18 | 25/04/2017 | LH | 08/06/2016 | Dickens Ladies Footwear (SL307) | Sales QE Credit | Credit note no CR10 | Trade Debtors (1100) | | 282.00 | No |
| | | | | | | | Sales - Ladies Footwear (4001) | 235.00 | | No |
| | | | | | | | VAT on Sales (2200) | 47.00 | | No |

From: 31/05/2016
To: 30/06/2016

Shoes 4U
Audit Trail Breakdown

25 Apr 2017
14:18

| | | | | | | | | | | |
|---|---|---|---|---|---|---|---|---|---|---|
| 19 | 25/04/2017 | LH | 02/06/2016 | Bootsy & Smudge Ltd (PL112) | Purchase QE Invoice | Inv B/752 | Trade Creditors (2100) | | 360.00 | No |
| | | | | | | | Purchases - Ladies Footwear (5001) | 300.00 | | No |
| | | | | | | | VAT on Purchases (2201) | 60.00 | | No |
| 20 | 25/04/2017 | LH | 10/06/2016 | Briggsthorpe Boots (PL168) | Purchase QE Invoice | Inv 12350 | Trade Creditors (2100) | | 3,000.00 | No |
| | | | | | | | Purchases - Men's Footwear (5000) | 2,500.00 | | No |
| | | | | | | | VAT on Purchases (2201) | 500.00 | | No |
| 21 | 25/04/2017 | LH | 12/06/2016 | Gallows Fashion (PL172) | Purchase QE Invoice | Inv G-2285 | Trade Creditors (2100) | | 3,000.00 | No |
| | | | | | | | Purchases - Men's Footwear (5000) | 2,500.00 | | No |
| | | | | | | | VAT on Purchases (2201) | 500.00 | | No |
| 22 | 25/04/2017 | LH | 13/06/2016 | Bootsy & Smudge Ltd (PL112) | Purchase QE Invoice | Inv B/753 | Trade Creditors (2100) | | 240.00 | No |
| | | | | | | | Purchases - Ladies Footwear (5001) | 200.00 | | No |
| | | | | | | | VAT on Purchases (2201) | 40.00 | | No |
| 23 | 25/04/2017 | LH | 11/06/2016 | Beckers Gate Ltd (SL166) | Customer Receipt | Chq no 198846 | Trade Debtors (1100) | | 4,811.88 | No |
| | | | | | | | Current (1200) | 4,811.88 | | Yes |
| 24 | 25/04/2017 | LH | 14/06/2016 | Eaton Bowls Club (SL213) | Customer Receipt | Chq No 107654 | Trade Debtors (1100) | | 961.98 | No |
| | | | | | | | Current (1200) | 961.98 | | Yes |
| 25 | 25/04/2017 | LH | 14/06/2016 | Jones Footwear (SL302) | Customer Receipt | 244536 | Trade Debtors (1100) | | 3,828.75 | No |
| | | | | | | | Current (1200) | 3,828.75 | | Yes |
| 26 | 25/04/2017 | LH | 18/06/2016 | Gallows Fashion (PL172) | Supplier Payment | Chq no 109887 | Trade Creditors (2100) | 400.00 | | No |
| | | | | | | | Current (1200) | | 400.00 | No |
| 27 | 25/04/2017 | LH | 18/06/2016 | Briggsthorpe Boots (PL168) | Supplier Payment | Chq no 109888 | Trade Creditors (2100) | 23,300.00 | | No |
| | | | | | | | Current (1200) | | 23,300.00 | Yes |
| 28 | 25/04/2017 | LH | 05/06/2016 | | Other Payment | Voucher no 010 | Cash (1210) | | 9.90 | No |
| | | | | | | | Refreshments (7502) | 9.90 | | No |
| 29 | 25/04/2017 | LH | 10/06/2016 | | Other Payment | Voucher no 011 | Cash (1210) | | 13.50 | No |
| | | | | | | | Office Stationery (7501) | 11.25 | | No |

| From: 31/05/2016 To: 30/06/2016 | | | | Shoes 4U Audit Trail Breakdown | | | | | | 25 Apr 2017 14:18 |
|---|---|---|---|---|---|---|---|---|---|---|
| | | | | | | VAT on Purchases (2201) | | 2.25 | | No |
| 30 | 25/04/2017 | LH | 10/06/2016 | Bank Transfer | TRF02 | Current (1200) | | | 23.40 | Yes |
| | | | | | | Cash (1210) | | 23.40 | | No |
| 31 | 25/04/2017 | LH | 23/06/2016 | Other Receipt | F027 | Sales - Men's Footwear (4000) | | | 64.66 | No |
| | | | | | | VAT on Sales (2200) | | | 12.93 | No |
| | | | | | | Current (1200) | | 77.59 | | Yes |
| 42 | 25/04/2017 | LH | 25/06/2016 | Journal | JNL 209 | Drawings - equity (3260) | 3,200.00 | | | No |
| | | | | | | Current (1200) | | | 3,200.00 | Yes |
| 43 | 25/04/2017 | LH | 22/06/2016 | Other Receipt | DC03 | Sales - Ladies Footwear (4001) | | | 45.00 | No |
| | | | | | | VAT on Sales (2200) | | | 9.00 | No |
| | | | | | | Current (1200) | | 54.00 | | Yes |

| From: 31/05/2016 To: 30/06/2016 | | | | Shoes 4U Audit Trail Breakdown | | | | | | 25 Apr 2017 14:18 |
|---|---|---|---|---|---|---|---|---|---|---|
| 44 | 25/04/2017 | LH | 25/06/2016 | Bank Payment | Bank Charge | Current (1200) | | | 50.00 | Yes |
| | | | | | | Bank charges and interest (7900) | | 50.00 | | No |
| 47 | 25/04/2017 | LH | 25/06/2016 | Other Receipt | Rent | Other income (4900) | | | 1,500.00 | No |
| | | | | | | Current (1200) | | 1,500.00 | | Yes |
| 48 | 25/04/2017 | LH | 25/06/2016 | Other Payment | Electricity | Current (1200) | | | 193.00 | Yes |
| | | | | | | Electricity (7200) | | 193.00 | | No |

## Task 15

## Nominal Ledger Activity Report for Trade Creditors and Sales – Ladies Footwear

| From: 31/05/2016 To: 30/06/2016 | | | | Shoes 4U Detailed Nominal Activity: Trade Creditors (2100) | | | | | | 25 Apr 2017 14:23 |
|---|---|---|---|---|---|---|---|---|---|---|

Transaction Type: All

| Trx No | Date | Invoice Number | Name | Type | Reference | Description | Debit | Credit | Running Total |
|---|---|---|---|---|---|---|---|---|---|
| | | | | | | Opening Balance | | 0.00 | |
| 5 | 31/05/2016 | | Bootsy & Smudge Ltd (PL112) | Supplier OB Invoice | Inv B/468 | | | 2,881.26 | 2,881.26 Cr |
| 6 | 31/05/2016 | | Briggsthorpe Boots (PL168) | Supplier OB Invoice | Inv 0001087 | | | 43,200.00 | 46,081.26 Cr |
| 7 | 31/05/2016 | | Gallows Fashion (PL172) | Supplier OB Invoice | Inv G-01239 | | | 400.00 | 46,481.26 Cr |
| 8 | 31/05/2016 | | Dickens Ladies Footwear (PL173) | Supplier OB Invoice | Inv 06345 | | | 567.00 | 47,048.26 Cr |
| 19 | 02/06/2016 | | Bootsy & Smudge Ltd (PL112) | Purchase QE Invoice | Inv B/752 | | | 360.00 | 47,408.26 Cr |
| 20 | 10/06/2016 | | Briggsthorpe Boots (PL168) | Purchase QE Invoice | Inv 12350 | | | 3,000.00 | 50,408.26 Cr |
| 21 | 12/06/2016 | | Gallows Fashion (PL172) | Purchase QE Invoice | Inv G-2285 | | | 3,000.00 | 53,408.26 Cr |
| 22 | 13/06/2016 | | Bootsy & Smudge Ltd (PL112) | Purchase QE Invoice | Inv B/753 | | | 240.00 | 53,648.26 Cr |
| 26 | 18/06/2016 | | Gallows Fashion (PL172) | Supplier Payment | Chq no 109887 | | 400.00 | | 53,248.26 Cr |
| 27 | 18/06/2016 | | Briggsthorpe Boots (PL168) | Supplier Payment | Chq no 109888 | | 23,300.00 | | 29,948.26 Cr |
| | | | | | | Closing Balance | | 29,948.26 | |
| | | | | | | Period Variance | | 29,948.26 | |

| From: 31/05/2016 To: 30/06/2016 | | | | Shoes 4U Detailed Nominal Activity: Sales - Ladies Footwear (4001) | | | | | | 25 Apr 2017 14:25 |
|---|---|---|---|---|---|---|---|---|---|---|

Transaction Type: All

| Trx No | Date | Invoice Number | Name | Type | Reference | Description | Debit | Credit | Running Total |
|---|---|---|---|---|---|---|---|---|---|
| | | | | | | Opening Balance | | 0.00 | |
| 11 | 31/05/2016 | | | Journal Opening Balance | OB 1/6/16 | (Opening Balance) | | 43,210.00 | 43,210.00 Cr |
| 18 | 08/06/2016 | | Dickens Ladies Footwear (SL307) | Sales QE Credit | Credit note no CR10 | | 235.00 | | 42,975.00 Cr |
| 16 | 14/06/2016 | | Dickens Ladies Footwear (SL307) | Sales QE Invoice | Inv 1624 | | | 1,850.00 | 44,825.00 Cr |
| 17 | 17/06/2016 | | Jones Footwear (SL302) | Sales QE Invoice | Inv 1625 | | | 1,175.75 | 46,000.75 Cr |
| 43 | 22/06/2016 | | | Other Receipt | DC03 | paid by debit card | | 45.00 | 46,045.75 Cr |
| | | | | | | Closing Balance | | 46,045.75 | |
| | | | | | | Period Variance | | 46,045.75 | |

## TASK 15

### Aged Debtors Analysis

| | | Shoes 4U | | | | | | 25 Apr 2017 |
|---|---|---|---|---|---|---|---|---|
| To: 30/06/2016 | | **Aged Debtors Breakdown** | | | | | | 14:27 |

| Date | Reference | Total | Due Date | O/S Amt | < 30 days | < 60 days | < 90 days | Older |
|---|---|---|---|---|---|---|---|---|
| Beckers Gate Ltd (SL186), Credit limit: £5,000.00 | | | | | | | | |
| , Terms: 30 days - OVERDUE | | | | | | | | |
| 04/06/2016 | QE-Inv 1622 | 540.00 | 04/07/2016 | 540.00 | 540.00 | | | |
| | | | | £540.00 | £540.00 | £0.00 | £0.00 | £0.00 |
| | | | | | | | | |
| Dickens Ladies Footwear (SL307), Credit limit: £11,000.00 | | | | | | | | |
| , Terms: 30 days - OVERDUE | | | | | | | | |
| 31/05/2016 | OB-Inv 1601 | 783.66 | 30/06/2016 | 783.66 | | 783.66 | | |
| 08/06/2016 | QE-Credit note no CR10 | -282.00 | | -282.00 | -282.00 | | | |
| 14/06/2016 | QE-Inv 1624 | 540.00 | 14/07/2016 | 540.00 | 540.00 | | | |
| 14/06/2016 | QE-Inv 1624 | 2,220.00 | 14/07/2016 | 2,220.00 | 2,220.00 | | | |
| | | | | £3,261.66 | £2,478.00 | £783.66 | £0.00 | £0.00 |
| | | | | | | | | |
| Eaton Bowls Club (SL213), Credit limit: £3,000.00 | | | | | | | | |
| , Terms: 30 days - OVERDUE | | | | | | | | |
| 06/06/2016 | QE-Inv 1623 | 1,662.00 | 06/07/2016 | 1,662.00 | 1,662.00 | | | |
| | | | | £1,662.00 | £1,662.00 | £0.00 | £0.00 | £0.00 |
| | | | | | | | | |
| Jones Footwear (SL302), Credit limit: £6,000.00 | | | | | | | | |
| , Terms: 30 days - OVERDUE | | | | | | | | |
| 17/06/2016 | QE-Inv 1625 | 1,410.90 | 17/07/2016 | 1,410.90 | 1,410.90 | | | |
| | | | | £1,410.90 | £1,410.90 | £0.00 | £0.00 | £0.00 |
| | | TOTAL | | £6,874.56 | £6,090.90 | £783.66 | £0.00 | £0.00 |

# PRACTICE PAPER 4

## SPORTS GEAR ANSWERS

### TASK 3.2

**Customer Address List**

| | Sports Gear | 25 Apr 2017 |
|---|---|---|
| | **Customer Address List** | 15:30 |

Address Types: All

| Customer Name | Address | Contact name | Phone | Mobile | Email | Fax |
|---|---|---|---|---|---|---|
| J Hollingham (SL01) | 56 Glencoe Avenue<br>Gants Hill<br>Ilford<br>Essex<br>IG1 6FR | Main Contact | | | | |
| Paul McCallum (SL02) | St Albans Road<br>Seven Kings<br>Essex<br>IG7 8DS | Main Contact | | | | |
| Kerry Jenkins (SL03) | 34 Gloucester Road<br>Gillingham<br>Kent<br>ME14 3TL | Main Contact | | | | |
| Harry Bucket (SL04) | 54 Dale Road<br>Harrogate<br>North Yorks<br>YO2 3HN | Main Contact | | | | |
| Evelyn Rose (SL05) | 98 Crabtree Drive<br>Bromley<br>Kent<br>DA3 6AY | Main Contact | | | | |

### TASK 3.2

**Supplier Address List**

| | Sports Gear | 25 Apr 2017 |
|---|---|---|
| | **Supplier Address List** | 15:31 |

Address Types: All

| Supplier Name | Address | Contact name | Phone | Mobile | Email | Fax |
|---|---|---|---|---|---|---|
| Radcliff and Sons (PL01) | Orient House<br>Lower Clapham<br>London<br>E1 2RH | Main Contact | | | | |
| Tennison Bros (PL02) | White Cottage<br>London<br>WC1 6YD | Main Contact | | | | |
| Skipton & Co (PL03) | 22 Chatsworth Lane<br>Water Square<br>London<br>EC1V 6NU | Main Contact | | | | |
| Evelyn Rose (PL04) | 98 Crabtree Drive<br>Bromley<br>Kent<br>DA3 6AY | Main Contact | | | | |

## TASK 3.2

## Trial Balance

From: 30/06/2016  
To:   31/07/2016

Sports Gear  
**Trial Balance Report**

25 Apr 2017  
15:28

This period only

| Nominal Code | Name | Selected Period | |
|---|---|---|---|
| | | Debit | Credit |
| 0030 | Office equipment - Cost | 8,430.00 | |
| 0040 | Fixtures and fittings - Cost | 18,000.00 | |
| 0050 | Motor Vehicles - Cost | 15,500.00 | |
| 1100 | Trade Debtors | 8,445.46 | |
| 1200 | Current | 3,325.40 | |
| 1210 | Cash | 300.00 | |
| 2100 | Trade Creditors | | 8,914.14 |
| 2200 | VAT on Sales | | 3,458.00 |
| 2201 | VAT on Purchases | 1,120.00 | |
| 3200 | Capital introduced | | 52,000.00 |
| 3260 | Drawings - equity | 1,294.00 | |
| 4000 | Sales - Tennis Racquets | | 13,266.78 |
| 4001 | Sales - Exercise Bikes | | 22,310.00 |
| 4002 | Sales - Golf Clubs | | 9,543.00 |
| 4003 | Sales - Fishing Rods | | 5,644.00 |
| 5000 | Purchases - Tennis Racquets | 21,354.00 | |
| 5001 | Purchases - Exercise Bikes | 25,610.00 | |
| 5002 | Purchases - Golf Clubs | 5,475.00 | |
| 5003 | Purchases - Fishing Rods | 4,796.00 | |
| 7200 | Electricity | 496.06 | |
| 7500 | Office Stationery | 430.00 | |
| 7501 | Postage | 560.00 | |
| | TOTAL | £115,135.92 | £115,135.92 |

## TASK 8

**Remittance Advices**

# Remittance Advice

Date Paid: 14/07/2016

Reference: PL01

**Radcliff and Sons**
Orient House
Lower Clapham
London
E1 2RH

**Sports Gear**
34 Hockey Avenue
Tennison
London
EC1V 1NY
United Kingdom

Telephone: 01234 567891

VAT Number: GB 123456789

**Reference:** Chq no 170012

| Our Ref | Your Ref | Date | Total Amount | Amount Paid |
|---------|----------|------|--------------|-------------|
| Inv 1874 | | 30/06/2016 | 5,362.14 | 5,362.14 |
| | | | **Total Paid:** | **£ 5,362.14 GBP** |

# Remittance Advice

Date Paid: 17/07/2016

Reference: PL02

**Tennison Bros**
White Cottage
London
WC1 6YD

**Sports Gear**
34 Hockey Avenue
Tennison
London
EC1V 1NY
United Kingdom

Telephone: 01234 567891

VAT Number: GB 123456789

**Reference:** Chq no 170013

| Our Ref | Your Ref | Date | Total Amount | Amount Paid |
|---------|----------|------|--------------|-------------|
| Inv B-321 | | 30/06/2016 | 2,801.00 | 2,801.00 |
| | | | **Total Paid:** | **£ 2,801.00 GBP** |

## TASK 11

### Trial Balance

From: 30/06/2016
To:  31/07/2016

Sports Gear
**Trial Balance Report**

25 Apr 2017
16:09

This period only

| Nominal Code | Name | Selected Period | |
|---|---|---|---|
| | | Debit | Credit |
| 0030 | Office equipment - Cost | 8,430.00 | |
| 0040 | Fixtures and fittings - Cost | 18,000.00 | |
| 0050 | Motor Vehicles - Cost | 15,500.00 | |
| 1100 | Trade Debtors | 6,108.50 | |
| 1200 | Current | 6,811.61 | |
| 1210 | Cash | | 132.16 |
| 2100 | Trade Creditors | | 3,629.46 |
| 2200 | VAT on Sales | | 5,010.07 |
| 2201 | VAT on Purchases | 1,662.62 | |
| 3200 | Capital introduced | | 52,000.00 |
| 3260 | Drawings - equity | 1,294.00 | |
| 4000 | Sales - Tennis Racquets | | 16,276.83 |
| 4001 | Sales - Exercise Bikes | | 25,222.47 |
| 4002 | Sales - Golf Clubs | | 11,056.80 |
| 4003 | Sales - Fishing Rods | | 5,968.00 |
| 5000 | Purchases - Tennis Racquets | 21,904.00 | |
| 5001 | Purchases - Exercise Bikes | 25,930.00 | |
| 5002 | Purchases - Golf Clubs | 6,303.55 | |
| 5003 | Purchases - Fishing Rods | 5,467.00 | |
| 7200 | Electricity | 496.06 | |
| 7500 | Office Stationery | 449.90 | |
| 7501 | Postage | 938.55 | |
| | **TOTAL** | **£119,295.79** | **£119,295.79** |

## TASK 11

### Sales Day Book

From: 30/06/2016        Sports Gear        25 Apr 2017
To:    31/07/2016        **Sales Day Book Report**        16:10

Type: Sales QE Invoice

| Trx No | Type | Date | Name | Invoice Number | Ref | Details | Net | VAT | Total |
|---|---|---|---|---|---|---|---|---|---|
| 13 | Sales QE Invoice | 04/07/2016 | J Hollingham | | Inv 1052 | | 882.00 | 176.40 | 1,058.40 |
| 14 | Sales QE Invoice | 04/07/2016 | J Hollingham | | Inv 1052 | | 1,023.60 | 204.72 | 1,228.32 |
| 15 | Sales QE Invoice | 04/07/2016 | J Hollingham | | Inv 1052 | | 324.00 | 64.80 | 388.80 |
| 16 | Sales QE Invoice | 06/07/2016 | Kerry Jenkins | | Inv 1053 | | 132.30 | 26.46 | 158.76 |
| 17 | Sales QE Invoice | 08/07/2016 | Harry Bucket | | Inv 1054 | | 1,513.80 | 302.76 | 1,816.56 |
| | | | | | | TOTAL | £3,875.70 | £775.14 | £4,650.84 |

## TASK 11

### Purchase Day Book

From: 30/06/2016        Sports Gear        25 Apr 2017
To:    31/07/2016        **Purchase Day Book Report**        16:11

Type: Purchase QE Invoice

| Trx No | Type | Date | Name | Invoice Number | Ref | Details | Net | VAT | Total |
|---|---|---|---|---|---|---|---|---|---|
| 19 | Purchase QE Invoice | 03/07/2016 | Radcliff and Sons | | Inv 1099 | | 550.00 | 110.00 | 660.00 |
| 20 | Purchase QE Invoice | 05/07/2016 | Tennison Bros | | Inv B-1147 | | 320.00 | 64.00 | 384.00 |
| 21 | Purchase QE Invoice | 05/07/2016 | Tennison Bros | | Inv B-1147 | | 35.00 | 0.00 | 35.00 |
| 22 | Purchase QE Invoice | 10/07/2016 | Skipton & Co | | Inv 2785 | | 938.00 | 187.60 | 1,125.60 |
| 23 | Purchase QE Invoice | 10/07/2016 | Evelyn Rose | | Inv A/5698 | | 671.00 | 134.20 | 805.20 |
| | | | | | | TOTAL | £2,514.00 | £495.80 | £3,009.80 |

## TASK 11

### Customer Activity Report

From: 30/06/2016
To:   31/07/2016

Sports Gear
**Customer Activity Report**

25 Apr 2017
16:12

**J Hollingham (SL01)**

| Date | Number | Reference | Type | Net | VAT | Total | Discount | Outstanding |
|---|---|---|---|---|---|---|---|---|
| 30/06/2016 | | Inv 1001 | Customer OB Invoice | 3,462.12 | 0.00 | 3,462.12 | | 0.00 |
| 04/07/2016 | | Inv 1052 | Sales QE Invoice | 882.00 | 176.40 | 1,058.40 | | 1,058.40 |
| 04/07/2016 | | Inv 1052 | Sales QE Invoice | 1,023.60 | 204.72 | 1,228.32 | | 1,228.32 |
| 04/07/2016 | | Inv 1052 | Sales QE Invoice | 324.00 | 64.80 | 388.80 | | 388.80 |
| 17/07/2016 | | CR34 | Sales QE Credit | -510.63 | -102.12 | -612.75 | | 0.00 |
| 19/07/2016 | | Chq no 542321 | Customer Receipt | | | -2,849.37 | 0.00 | 0.00 |
| | | | | | | 2,675.52 | | 2,675.52 |

**Paul McCallum (SL02)**

| Date | Number | Reference | Type | Net | VAT | Total | Discount | Outstanding |
|---|---|---|---|---|---|---|---|---|
| 30/06/2016 | | Inv 0087 | Customer OB Invoice | 514.68 | 0.00 | 514.68 | | 514.68 |
| | | | | | | 514.68 | | 514.68 |

**Kerry Jenkins (SL03)**

| Date | Number | Reference | Type | Net | VAT | Total | Discount | Outstanding |
|---|---|---|---|---|---|---|---|---|
| 30/06/2016 | | Inv 0093 | Customer OB Invoice | 758.34 | 0.00 | 758.34 | | 0.00 |
| 06/07/2016 | | Inv 1053 | Sales QE Invoice | 132.30 | 26.46 | 158.76 | | 158.76 |
| 12/07/2016 | | Chq no 222547 | Customer Receipt | | | -758.34 | 0.00 | 0.00 |
| | | | | | | 158.76 | | 158.76 |

**Harry Bucket (SL04)**

| Date | Number | Reference | Type | Net | VAT | Total | Discount | Outstanding |
|---|---|---|---|---|---|---|---|---|
| 30/06/2016 | | Inv 1003 | Customer OB Invoice | 2,767.34 | 0.00 | 2,767.34 | | 0.00 |
| 08/07/2016 | | Inv 1054 | Sales QE Invoice | 1,513.80 | 302.76 | 1,816.56 | | 1,816.56 |
| 13/07/2016 | | BACS | Customer Receipt | | | -2,767.34 | 0.00 | 0.00 |
| | | | | | | 1,816.56 | | 1,816.56 |

**Evelyn Rose (SL05)**

| Date | Number | Reference | Type | Net | VAT | Total | Discount | Outstanding |
|---|---|---|---|---|---|---|---|---|

Who: Leanne Halsall                    Produced by Sage One                    Page 1 of 2

From: 30/06/2016
To:   31/07/2016

Sports Gear
**Customer Activity Report**

25 Apr 2017
16:12

| Date | Number | Reference | Type | Net | VAT | Total | Discount | Outstanding |
|---|---|---|---|---|---|---|---|---|
| 30/06/2016 | | Inv 1004 | Customer OB Invoice | 942.98 | 0.00 | 942.98 | | 942.98 |
| | | | | | | 942.98 | | 942.98 |

## TASK 11

### Supplier Activity Report

#### Radcliff and Sons (PL01)

| Date | Number | Reference | Type | Net | VAT | Total | Discount | Outstanding |
|------|--------|-----------|------|-----|-----|-------|----------|-------------|
| 30/06/2016 | | Inv 1874 | Supplier OB Invoice | 5,362.14 | 0.00 | 5,362.14 | | 0.00 |
| 03/07/2016 | | Inv 1099 | Purchase QE Invoice | 550.00 | 110.00 | 660.00 | | 660.00 |
| 14/07/2016 | | Chq no 170012 | Supplier Payment | | | -5,362.14 | 0.00 | 0.00 |
| | | | | | | 660.00 | | 660.00 |

#### Tennison Bros (PL02)

| Date | Number | Reference | Type | Net | VAT | Total | Discount | Outstanding |
|------|--------|-----------|------|-----|-----|-------|----------|-------------|
| 30/06/2016 | | Inv B-321 | Supplier OB Invoice | 2,801.00 | 0.00 | 2,801.00 | | 0.00 |
| 05/07/2016 | | Inv B-1147 | Purchase QE Invoice | 35.00 | 0.00 | 35.00 | | 35.00 |
| 05/07/2016 | | Inv B-1147 | Purchase QE Invoice | 320.00 | 64.00 | 384.00 | | 384.00 |
| 17/07/2016 | | Chq no 170013 | Supplier Payment | | | -2,801.00 | 0.00 | 0.00 |
| | | | | | | 419.00 | | 419.00 |

#### Skipton & Co (PL03)

| Date | Number | Reference | Type | Net | VAT | Total | Discount | Outstanding |
|------|--------|-----------|------|-----|-----|-------|----------|-------------|
| 30/06/2016 | | Inv 1087 | Supplier OB Invoice | 501.00 | 0.00 | 501.00 | | 501.00 |
| 10/07/2016 | | Inv 2785 | Purchase QE Invoice | 938.00 | 187.60 | 1,125.60 | | 1,125.60 |
| 19/07/2016 | | CX432 | Purchase QE Credit | -109.45 | -21.89 | -131.34 | | -131.34 |
| | | | | | | 1,495.26 | | 1,495.26 |

#### Evelyn Rose (PL04)

| Date | Number | Reference | Type | Net | VAT | Total | Discount | Outstanding |
|------|--------|-----------|------|-----|-----|-------|----------|-------------|
| 30/06/2016 | | Inv A193 | Supplier OB Invoice | 250.00 | 0.00 | 250.00 | | 250.00 |
| 10/07/2016 | | Inv A/5698 | Purchase QE Invoice | 671.00 | 134.20 | 805.20 | | 805.20 |
| | | | | | | 1,055.20 | | 1,055.20 |

## TASK 11

## Aged Creditors Report

Sports Gear
**Aged Creditors Breakdown**

| Date | Reference | Total | Due Date | O/S Amt | < 30 days | < 60 days | < 90 days | Older |
|---|---|---|---|---|---|---|---|---|
| Evelyn Rose (PL04), Credit limit: £3,000.00 | | | | | | | | |
| , Terms: 30 days - OVERDUE | | | | | | | | |
| 10/07/2016 | Inv A/5698 | 805.20 | 09/08/2016 | 805.20 | 805.20 | | | |
| 30/06/2016 | Inv A193 | 250.00 | 30/07/2016 | 250.00 | | 250.00 | | |
| | | | | £1,055.20 | £805.20 | £250.00 | £0.00 | £0.00 |
| Radcliff and Sons (PL01), Credit limit: £15,500.00 | | | | | | | | |
| , Terms: 30 days - OVERDUE | | | | | | | | |
| 03/07/2016 | Inv 1099 | 660.00 | 02/08/2016 | 660.00 | 660.00 | | | |
| | | | | £660.00 | £660.00 | £0.00 | £0.00 | £0.00 |
| Skipton & Co (PL03), Credit limit: £9,000.00 | | | | | | | | |
| , Terms: 30 days - OVERDUE | | | | | | | | |
| 19/07/2016 | CX432 | -131.34 | | -131.34 | -131.34 | | | |
| 30/06/2016 | Inv 1087 | 501.00 | 30/07/2016 | 501.00 | | 501.00 | | |
| 10/07/2016 | Inv 2785 | 1,125.60 | 09/08/2016 | 1,125.60 | 1,125.60 | | | |
| | | | | £1,495.26 | £994.26 | £501.00 | £0.00 | £0.00 |
| Tennison Bros (PL02), Credit limit: £11,000.00 | | | | | | | | |
| , Terms: 30 days - OVERDUE | | | | | | | | |
| 05/07/2016 | Inv B-1147 | 384.00 | 04/08/2016 | 384.00 | 384.00 | | | |
| 05/07/2016 | Inv B-1147 | 35.00 | 04/08/2016 | 35.00 | 35.00 | | | |
| | | | | £419.00 | £419.00 | £0.00 | £0.00 | £0.00 |
| | | | TOTAL | £3,629.46 | £2,878.46 | £751.00 | £0.00 | £0.00 |

## TASK 11

### Aged Debtors Report

| | | | | Sports Gear | | | | 25 Apr 2017 |
|---|---|---|---|---|---|---|---|---|
| To: 31/07/2016 | | | | **Aged Debtors Breakdown** | | | | 16:16 |

| Date | Reference | Total | Due Date | O/S Amt | < 30 days | < 60 days | < 90 days | Older |
|---|---|---|---|---|---|---|---|---|
| Evelyn Rose (SL05), Credit limit: £7,000.00 | | | | | | | | |
| , Terms: 30 days - OVERDUE | | | | | | | | |
| 30/06/2016 | OB-Inv 1004 | 942.98 | 30/07/2016 | 942.98 | | 942.98 | | |
| | | | | £942.98 | £0.00 | £942.98 | £0.00 | £0.00 |
| Harry Bucket (SL04), Credit limit: £12,000.00 | | | | | | | | |
| , Terms: 30 days - OVERDUE | | | | | | | | |
| 08/07/2016 | QE-Inv 1054 | 1,816.56 | 07/08/2016 | 1,816.56 | 1,816.56 | | | |
| | | | | £1,816.56 | £1,816.56 | £0.00 | £0.00 | £0.00 |
| J Hollingham (SL01), Credit limit: £5,000.00 | | | | | | | | |
| , Terms: 30 days - OVERDUE | | | | | | | | |
| 04/07/2016 | QE-Inv 1052 | 1,058.40 | 03/08/2016 | 1,058.40 | 1,058.40 | | | |
| 04/07/2016 | QE-Inv 1052 | 1,228.32 | 03/08/2016 | 1,228.32 | 1,228.32 | | | |
| 04/07/2016 | QE-Inv 1052 | 388.80 | 03/08/2016 | 388.80 | 388.80 | | | |
| | | | | £2,675.52 | £2,675.52 | £0.00 | £0.00 | £0.00 |
| Kerry Jenkins (SL03), Credit limit: £8,000.00 | | | | | | | | |
| , Terms: 30 days - OVERDUE | | | | | | | | |
| 06/07/2016 | QE-Inv 1053 | 158.76 | 05/08/2016 | 158.76 | 158.76 | | | |
| | | | | £158.76 | £158.76 | £0.00 | £0.00 | £0.00 |
| Paul McCallum (SL02), Credit limit: £9,500.00 | | | | | | | | |
| , Terms: 30 days - OVERDUE | | | | | | | | |
| 30/06/2016 | OB-Inv 0087 | 514.68 | 30/07/2016 | 514.68 | | 514.68 | | |
| | | | | £514.68 | £0.00 | £514.68 | £0.00 | £0.00 |
| | | | TOTAL | £6,108.50 | £4,650.84 | £1,457.66 | £0.00 | £0.00 |

## TASK 11

### Customer Statement

From: 30/06/2016
To:     31/07/2016

Sports Gear
**Statement Summary Report**

25 Apr 2017
16:17

**Paul McCallum (SL02)**
St Albans Road
Seven Kings
Essex
IG7 8DS

| Date | Activity | Invoices | Payments | Balance |
|------|----------|----------|----------|---------|
| 30/06/2016 | Sales Invoice | 514.68 | 0.00 | 514.68 |

| Summary | | | | |
|---------|--|--|--|--|
| Overdue | | | | 514.68 |

## Task 13

### Customer change of address

## TASK 18

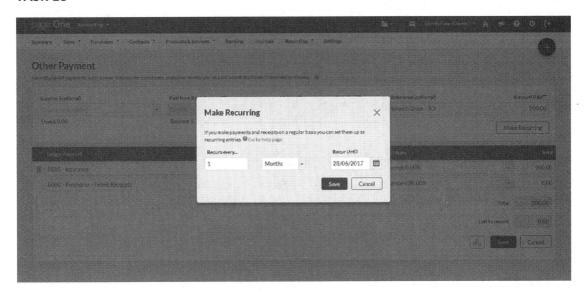

## TASK 21

## Customer Address List

| Customer Name | Address | Contact name | Phone | Mobile | Email | Fax |
|---|---|---|---|---|---|---|
| J Hollingham (SL01) | 56 Glencoe Avenue<br>Gants Hill<br>Ilford<br>Essex<br>IG1 6FR | Main Contact | | | | |
| Paul McCallum (SL02) | St Albans Road<br>Seven Kings<br>Essex<br>IG7 8DS | Main Contact | | | | |
| Kerry Jenkins (SL03) | 34 Gloucester Road<br>Gillingham<br>Kent<br>ME14 3TL | Main Contact | | | | |
| Harry Bucket (SL04) | 137 Chester Road<br>Capel Corner<br>CR3 2SA | Main Contact | 08459 754 256 | | | |
| Evelyn Rose (SL05) | 96 Crabtree Drive<br>Bromley<br>Kent<br>DA3 6AY | Main Contact | | | | |

Sports Gear
Customer Address List

27 Apr 2017
10:48

Address Types: All

## TASK 21

## Customer Activity (detailed report)

**J Hollingham (SL01)**

| Date | Number | Reference | Type | Net | VAT | Total | Discount | Outstanding |
|---|---|---|---|---|---|---|---|---|
| 30/06/2016 | | Inv 1001 | Customer OB Invoice | 3,462.12 | 0.00 | 3,462.12 | | 0.00 |
| 04/07/2016 | | Inv 1052 | Sales QE Invoice | 882.00 | 176.40 | 1,058.40 | | 0.00 |
| 04/07/2016 | | Inv 1052 | Sales QE Invoice | 1,023.60 | 204.72 | 1,228.32 | | 0.00 |
| 04/07/2016 | | Inv 1052 | Sales QE Invoice | 324.00 | 64.80 | 388.80 | | 0.00 |
| 17/07/2016 | | CR34 | Sales QE Credit | -510.63 | -102.12 | -612.75 | | 0.00 |
| 19/07/2016 | | Chq no 542321 | Customer Receipt | | | -2,849.37 | 0.00 | 0.00 |
| 28/07/2016 | | Chq no 087651 | Customer Receipt | | | -2,675.52 | 0.00 | 0.00 |
| | | | | | | 0.00 | | 0.00 |

**Paul McCallum (SL02)**

| Date | Number | Reference | Type | Net | VAT | Total | Discount | Outstanding |
|---|---|---|---|---|---|---|---|---|
| 30/06/2016 | | Inv 0087 | Customer OB Invoice | 514.68 | 0.00 | 514.68 | | 514.68 |
| | | | | | | 514.68 | | 514.68 |

**Kerry Jenkins (SL03)**

| Date | Number | Reference | Type | Net | VAT | Total | Discount | Outstanding |
|---|---|---|---|---|---|---|---|---|
| 30/06/2016 | | Inv 0093 | Customer OB Invoice | 758.34 | 0.00 | 758.34 | | 0.00 |
| 06/07/2016 | | Inv 1053 | Sales QE Invoice | 132.30 | 26.46 | 158.76 | | 158.76 |
| 12/07/2016 | | Chq no 222547 | Customer Receipt | | | -758.34 | 0.00 | 0.00 |
| | | | | | | 158.76 | | 158.76 |

**Harry Bucket (SL04)**

| Date | Number | Reference | Type | Net | VAT | Total | Discount | Outstanding |
|---|---|---|---|---|---|---|---|---|
| 30/06/2016 | | Inv 1003 | Customer OB Invoice | 2,767.34 | 0.00 | 2,767.34 | | 0.00 |
| 08/07/2016 | | Inv 1054 | Sales QE Invoice | 1,513.80 | 302.76 | 1,816.56 | | 1,316.56 |
| 13/07/2016 | | BACS | Customer Receipt | | | -2,767.34 | 0.00 | 0.00 |
| 28/07/2016 | | Chq no 198871 | Customer Receipt | | | -500.00 | 0.00 | 0.00 |
| | | | | | | 1,316.56 | | 1,316.56 |

Who: Leanne Halsall     Produced by Sage One     Page 1 of 2

**Evelyn Rose (SL05)**

| Date | Number | Reference | Type | Net | VAT | Total | Discount | Outstanding |
|---|---|---|---|---|---|---|---|---|
| 30/06/2016 | | Inv 1004 | Customer OB Invoice | 942.98 | 0.00 | 942.98 | | 942.98 |
| | | | | | | 942.98 | | 942.98 |

## TASK 21

### Supplier Activity (detailed report)

From: 30/06/2016
To:    31/07/2016

**Sports Gear**
**Supplier Activity Report**

27 Apr 2017
10:52

**Radcliff and Sons (PL01)**

| Date | Number | Reference | Type | Net | VAT | Total | Discount | Outstanding |
|------|--------|-----------|------|-----|-----|-------|----------|-------------|
| 30/06/2016 | | Inv 1874 | Supplier OB Invoice | 5,362.14 | 0.00 | 5,362.14 | | 0.00 |
| 03/07/2016 | | Inv 1099 | Purchase QE Invoice | 550.00 | 110.00 | 660.00 | | 0.00 |
| 14/07/2016 | | Chq no 170012 | Supplier Payment | | | -5,362.14 | 0.00 | 0.00 |
| 28/07/2016 | | Chq no 170015 | Supplier Payment | | | -660.00 | 0.00 | 0.00 |
| | | | | | | 0.00 | | 0.00 |

**Tennison Bros (PL02)**

| Date | Number | Reference | Type | Net | VAT | Total | Discount | Outstanding |
|------|--------|-----------|------|-----|-----|-------|----------|-------------|
| 30/06/2016 | | Inv B-321 | Supplier OB Invoice | 2,801.00 | 0.00 | 2,801.00 | | 0.00 |
| 05/07/2016 | | Inv B-1147 | Purchase QE Invoice | 35.00 | 0.00 | 35.00 | | 35.00 |
| 05/07/2016 | | Inv B-1147 | Purchase QE Invoice | 320.00 | 64.00 | 384.00 | | 384.00 |
| 17/07/2016 | | Chq no 170013 | Supplier Payment | | | -2,801.00 | 0.00 | 0.00 |
| | | | | | | 419.00 | | 419.00 |

**Skipton & Co (PL03)**

| Date | Number | Reference | Type | Net | VAT | Total | Discount | Outstanding |
|------|--------|-----------|------|-----|-----|-------|----------|-------------|
| 30/06/2016 | | Inv 1087 | Supplier OB Invoice | 501.00 | 0.00 | 501.00 | | 0.00 |
| 10/07/2016 | | Inv 2785 | Purchase QE Invoice | 938.00 | 187.60 | 1,125.60 | | 1,125.60 |
| 19/07/2016 | | CX432 | Purchase QE Credit | -109.45 | -21.89 | -131.34 | | -131.34 |
| 28/07/2016 | | Chq no 170014 | Supplier Payment | | | -501.00 | 0.00 | 0.00 |
| | | | | | | 994.26 | | 994.26 |

**Evelyn Rose (PL04)**

| Date | Number | Reference | Type | Net | VAT | Total | Discount | Outstanding |
|------|--------|-----------|------|-----|-----|-------|----------|-------------|
| 30/06/2016 | | Inv A193 | Supplier OB Invoice | 250.00 | 0.00 | 250.00 | | 250.00 |
| 10/07/2016 | | Inv A/5698 | Purchase QE Invoice | 671.00 | 134.20 | 805.20 | | 805.20 |
| | | | | | | 1,055.20 | | 1,055.20 |

## TASK 21

### Trial Balance for July

From: 30/06/2016
To:    31/07/2016

Sports Gear
**Trial Balance Report**

27 Apr 2017
10:56

This period only

| Nominal Code | Name | Selected Period | |
|---|---|---|---|
| | | Debit | Credit |
| 0030 | Office equipment - Cost | 8,430.00 | |
| 0040 | Fixtures and fittings - Cost | 18,000.00 | |
| 0050 | Motor Vehicles - Cost | 15,500.00 | |
| 1100 | Trade Debtors | 2,932.98 | |
| 1200 | Current | 4,924.78 | |
| 1210 | Cash | 300.00 | |
| 2100 | Trade Creditors | | 2,468.46 |
| 2200 | VAT on Sales | | 5,027.40 |
| 2201 | VAT on Purchases | 1,662.62 | |
| 3200 | Capital introduced | | 52,000.00 |
| 3260 | Drawings - equity | 4,735.00 | |
| 4000 | Sales - Tennis Racquets | | 16,318.50 |
| 4001 | Sales - Exercise Bikes | | 25,222.47 |
| 4002 | Sales - Golf Clubs | | 11,101.80 |
| 4003 | Sales - Fishing Rods | | 5,968.00 |
| 5000 | Purchases - Tennis Racquets | 21,904.00 | |
| 5001 | Purchases - Exercise Bikes | 25,930.00 | |
| 5002 | Purchases - Golf Clubs | 6,303.55 | |
| 5003 | Purchases - Fishing Rods | 5,467.00 | |
| 7200 | Electricity | 496.06 | |
| 7500 | Office Stationery | 449.90 | |
| 7501 | Postage | 938.55 | |
| 7610 | Insurance | 100.00 | |
| 7900 | Bank charges and interest | 32.19 | |
| | TOTAL | £118,106.63 | £118,106.63 |

## TASK 21

## Nominal Ledger Activity Report for Bank/Petty Cash

From: 30/06/2016
To:  31/07/2016

Sports Gear
**Detailed Nominal Activity: Current (1200)**

27 Apr 2017
10:59

Transaction Type: All

| Trx No | Date | Invoice Number | Name | Type | Reference | Description | Debit | Credit | Running Total |
|---|---|---|---|---|---|---|---|---|---|
| | | | | | | Opening Balance | | 0.00 | |
| 10 | 30/06/2016 | | | Bank Opening Balance | | | 3,325.40 | | 3,325.40 Dr |
| 27 | 12/07/2016 | | Kerry Jenkins (SL03) | Customer Receipt | Chq no 222547 | | 758.34 | | 4,083.74 Dr |
| 28 | 13/07/2016 | | Harry Bucket (SL04) | Customer Receipt | BACS | | 2,767.34 | | 6,851.08 Dr |
| 33 | 13/07/2016 | | | Other Receipt | REC101 | | 1,200.00 | | 8,051.08 Dr |
| 29 | 14/07/2016 | | Radcliff and Sons (PL01) | Supplier Payment | Chq no 170012 | | | 5,362.14 | 2,688.94 Dr |
| 41 | 14/07/2016 | | | Other Receipt | ST5 | | 50.00 | | 2,738.94 Dr |
| 34 | 15/07/2016 | | | Other Receipt | REC102 | | 2,879.40 | | 5,618.34 Dr |
| 35 | 15/07/2016 | | | Other Receipt | REC103 | | 1,194.90 | | 6,813.24 Dr |
| 30 | 17/07/2016 | | Tennison Bros (PL02) | Supplier Payment | Chq no 170013 | | | 2,801.00 | 4,012.24 Dr |
| 26 | 19/07/2016 | | J Hollingham (SL01) | Customer Receipt | Chq no 542321 | | 2,849.37 | | 6,861.61 Dr |
| 42 | 19/07/2016 | | | Other Receipt | Debit card | | 54.00 | | 6,915.61 Dr |
| 36 | 25/07/2016 | | | Journal | JNL004 | | | 3,441.00 | 3,474.61 Dr |
| 37 | 28/07/2016 | | Skipton & Co (PL03) | Supplier Payment | Chq no 170014 | | | 501.00 | 2,973.61 Dr |
| 38 | 28/07/2016 | | Radcliff and Sons (PL01) | Supplier Payment | Chq no 170015 | | | 660.00 | 2,313.61 Dr |
| 39 | 28/07/2016 | | J Hollingham (SL01) | Customer Receipt | Chq no 087651 | | 2,675.52 | | 4,989.13 Dr |
| 40 | 28/07/2016 | | Harry Bucket (SL04) | Customer Receipt | Chq no 198871 | | 500.00 | | 5,489.13 Dr |
| 44 | 28/07/2016 | | | Other Payment | Ipswich Union - SO | | | 100.00 | 5,389.13 Dr |
| 53 | 31/07/2016 | | | Bank Payment | Bank Charge | | | 32.19 | 5,356.94 Dr |
| 54 | 31/07/2016 | | | Bank Transfer | TRF01 | | | 432.16 | 4,924.78 Dr |
| | | | | | | Closing Balance | 4,924.78 | | |
| | | | | | | Period Variance | 4,924.78 | | |

From: 30/06/2016
To:  31/07/2016

Sports Gear
**Detailed Nominal Activity: Cash (1210)**

27 Apr 2017
11:01

Transaction Type: All

| Trx No | Date | Invoice Number | Name | Type | Reference | Description | Debit | Credit | Running Total |
|---|---|---|---|---|---|---|---|---|---|
| | | | | | | Opening Balance | | 0.00 | |
| 11 | 30/06/2016 | | | Bank Opening Balance | | | 300.00 | | 300.00 Dr |
| 31 | 10/07/2016 | | | Other Payment | Voucher no 152 | | | 19.90 | 280.10 Dr |
| 32 | 20/07/2016 | | | Other Payment | Voucher no 187 | | | 412.26 | 132.16 Cr |
| 54 | 31/07/2016 | | | Bank Transfer | TRF01 | | 432.16 | | 300.00 Dr |
| | | | | | | Closing Balance | 300.00 | | |
| | | | | | | Period Variance | 300.00 | | |

# PRACTICE PAPER 5

## WAY TO WORK ANSWERS

### TASK 3.3

**Customer Address List**

| | | | | | | |
|---|---|---|---|---|---|---|
| | | | Way To Work | | 11 May 2017 | |
| | | | Customer Address List | | 14:14 | |

Address Types: All

| Customer Name | Address | Contact name | Phone | Mobile | Email | Fax |
|---|---|---|---|---|---|---|
| Morgan, Smith & Winston (JP01) | City Road<br>Islington<br>London<br>N1 9PL | Main Contact | | | | |
| Cyril West (JP02) | Grays West<br>Grays Inn Road<br>London<br>WC1 1LT | Main Contact | | | | |
| Wallace & Gromit Ltd (JP03) | 134 Upper Street<br>Islington<br>London<br>N1 2PT | Main Contact | | | | |
| Star Paper (JP04) | 66 White Lion Street<br>London<br>N1 5RX | Main Contact | | | | |

### TASK 3.3

**Supplier Address List**

| | | | | | | |
|---|---|---|---|---|---|---|
| | | | Way To Work | | 11 May 2017 | |
| | | | Supplier Address List | | 14:21 | |

Address Types: All

| Supplier Name | Address | Contact name | Phone | Mobile | Email | Fax |
|---|---|---|---|---|---|---|
| Paper Products UK (SP01) | South Down Trading Estate<br>Sheffield<br>S15 4DR | Main Contact | | | | |
| Wallace & Gromit Ltd (SP02) | 134 Upper Street<br>Islington<br>London<br>N1 2PT | Main Contact | | | | |
| Whole Office Furniture (SP03) | 176 East Way<br>Leeds<br>LD4 6PP | Main Contact | | | | |
| Stationery World (SP04) | 32 Great Portland Road<br>London<br>WC1V 6HH | Main Contact | | | | |

## TASK 3.3

### Trial Balance

Way To Work
**Trial Balance Report**

This period only

| Nominal Code | Name | | Selected Period | |
| --- | --- | --- | --- | --- |
| | | | Debit | Credit |
| 0040 | Fixtures and fittings - Cost | | 8,000.00 | |
| 0050 | Motor Vehicles - Cost | | 14,000.00 | |
| 1100 | Trade Debtors | | 9,173.68 | |
| 1200 | Current | | 4,710.81 | |
| 1210 | Cash | | 100.00 | |
| 1220 | Deposit | | 1,500.00 | |
| 2100 | Trade Creditors | | | 18,535.76 |
| 3200 | Capital introduced | | | 34,000.00 |
| 3260 | Drawings - equity | | 1,000.00 | |
| 4000 | Stationery Sales | | | 903.73 |
| 4001 | CD Rom Sales | | | 855.00 |
| 4002 | Printer Accessories Sales | | | 9,842.00 |
| 5000 | Stationery Purchases | | 2,400.00 | |
| 5001 | CD Rom Purchases | | 210.00 | |
| 5002 | Printer Accessory Purchases | | 15,000.00 | |
| 7000 | Wages and Salaries | | 5,600.00 | |
| 7100 | Rent and rates | | 2,100.00 | |
| 8200 | General Expenses | | 342.00 | |
| | | TOTAL | £64,136.49 | £64,136.49 |

**TASK 9**

# Remittance Advice

Date Paid: 31/03/2016

Reference: SP01

| Paper Products UK | | | | | Way To Work |
| South Down Trading Estate | | | | | 55 Upper Street |
| Sheffield | | | | | London |
| S15 4DR | | | | | N1 9PE |
| | | | | | United Kingdom |

Telephone: 01234 567891

VAT Number: GB 123456789

Reference: Chq no 100076

| Our Ref | Your Ref | Date | Total Amount | Amount Paid |
|---------|----------|------|--------------|-------------|
| Inv 0165 | | 29/02/2016 | 445.23 | 445.23 |
| | | **Total Paid:** | | **£ 445.23 GBP** |

**Task 9**

# Remittance Advice

Date Paid: 31/03/2016

Reference: SP03

| Whole Office Furniture | | | | | Way To Work |
| 176 East Way | | | | | 55 Upper Street |
| Leeds | | | | | London |
| LD4 6PP | | | | | N1 9PE |
| | | | | | United Kingdom |

Telephone: 01234 567891

VAT Number: GB 123456789

Reference: Chq no 100077

| Our Ref | Your Ref | Date | Total Amount | Amount Paid |
|---------|----------|------|--------------|-------------|
| Inv 1028 | | 29/02/2016 | 1,875.21 | 1,875.21 |
| | | **Total Paid:** | | **£ 1,875.21 GBP** |

**Task 9**

# Remittance Advice

Date Paid: 31/03/2016

Reference: SP04

| | Way To Work |
|---|---|
| **Stationery World**<br>32 Great Portland Road<br>London<br>WC1V 6HH | 55 Upper Street<br>London<br>N1 9PE<br>United Kingdom<br><br>Telephone: 01234 567891<br><br>VAT Number: GB 123456789 |

**Reference:** Chq no 100078

| Our Ref | Your Ref | Date | Total Amount | Amount Paid |
|---|---|---|---|---|
| Inv 0187 | | 29/02/2016 | 9,504.32 | 9,504.32 |
| | | | **Total Paid:** | **£ 9,504.32 GBP** |

# TASK 13

## Recurring payment

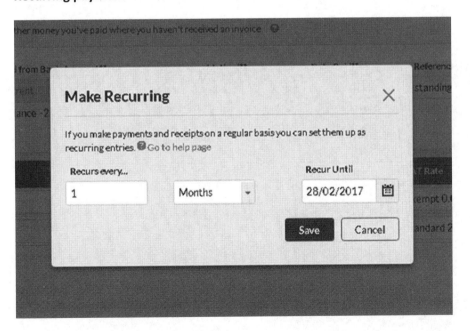

## TASK 15

## Customer Activity (detailed report)

From: 29/02/2016
To:    31/03/2016

**Way To Work**
**Customer Activity Report**

11 May 2017
15:38

### Morgan, Smith & Winston (JP01)

| Date | Number | Reference | Type | Net | VAT | Total | Discount | Outstanding |
|---|---|---|---|---|---|---|---|---|
| 29/02/2016 | | INV021 | Customer OB Invoice | 1,172.34 | 0.00 | 1,172.34 | | 0.00 |
| 05/03/2016 | | INV043 | Sales QE Invoice | 4,376.00 | 875.20 | 5,251.20 | | 5,251.20 |
| 07/03/2016 | | INV45 | Sales QE Invoice | 6,210.00 | 1,242.00 | 7,452.00 | | 7,452.00 |
| 15/03/2016 | | Chqno 203998 | Customer Receipt | | | -1,172.34 | 0.00 | 0.00 |
| | | | | | | 12,703.20 | | 12,703.20 |

### Cyril West (JP02)

| Date | Number | Reference | Type | Net | VAT | Total | Discount | Outstanding |
|---|---|---|---|---|---|---|---|---|
| 29/02/2016 | | INV045 | Customer OB Invoice | 2,954.00 | 0.00 | 2,954.00 | | 0.00 |
| 03/03/2016 | | INV041 | Sales QE Invoice | 780.00 | 156.00 | 936.00 | | 936.00 |
| 17/03/2016 | | Chq no 103112 | Customer Receipt | | | -2,954.00 | 0.00 | 0.00 |
| | | | | | | 936.00 | | 936.00 |

### Wallace & Gromit Ltd (JP03)

| Date | Number | Reference | Type | Net | VAT | Total | Discount | Outstanding |
|---|---|---|---|---|---|---|---|---|
| 29/02/2016 | | INV033 | Customer OB Invoice | 3,180.00 | 0.00 | 3,180.00 | | 3,180.00 |
| 07/03/2016 | | INV044 | Sales QE Invoice | 458.00 | 91.60 | 549.60 | | 549.60 |
| | | | | | | 3,729.60 | | 3,729.60 |

### Star Paper (JP04)

| Date | Number | Reference | Type | Net | VAT | Total | Discount | Outstanding |
|---|---|---|---|---|---|---|---|---|
| 29/02/2016 | | INV034 | Customer OB Invoice | 1,867.34 | 0.00 | 1,867.34 | | 0.00 |
| 03/03/2016 | | INV042 | Sales QE Invoice | 921.00 | 184.20 | 1,105.20 | | 1,105.20 |
| 17/03/2016 | | CR51 | Sales QE Credit | -251.27 | -50.25 | -301.52 | | 0.00 |
| 19/03/2016 | | Chq no 011211 | Customer Receipt | | | -1,565.82 | 0.00 | 0.00 |
| | | | | | | 1,105.20 | | 1,105.20 |

## TASK 15

### Supplier Activity (detailed report)

From: 29/02/2016

To:   31/03/2016

Way To Work
**Supplier Activity Report**

11 May 2017

15:42

**Paper Products UK (SP01)**

| Date | Number | Reference | Type | Net | VAT | Total | Discount | Outstanding |
|---|---|---|---|---|---|---|---|---|
| 29/02/2016 | | Inv 0165 | Supplier OB Invoice | 445.23 | 0.00 | 445.23 | | 0.00 |
| 10/03/2016 | | 0200 | Purchase QE Invoice | 489.00 | 97.80 | 586.80 | | 586.80 |
| 31/03/2016 | | Chq no 100076 | Supplier Payment | | | -445.23 | 0.00 | 0.00 |
| | | | | | | 586.80 | | 586.80 |

**Wallace & Gromit Ltd (SP02)**

| Date | Number | Reference | Type | Net | VAT | Total | Discount | Outstanding |
|---|---|---|---|---|---|---|---|---|
| 29/02/2016 | | Inv 02183 | Supplier OB Invoice | 6,711.00 | 0.00 | 6,711.00 | | 6,711.00 |
| 11/03/2016 | | 02241 | Purchase QE Invoice | 345.00 | 69.00 | 414.00 | | 414.00 |
| | | | | | | 7,125.00 | | 7,125.00 |

**Whole Office Furniture (SP03)**

| Date | Number | Reference | Type | Net | VAT | Total | Discount | Outstanding |
|---|---|---|---|---|---|---|---|---|
| 29/02/2016 | | Inv 1028 | Supplier OB Invoice | 1,875.21 | 0.00 | 1,875.21 | | 0.00 |
| 11/03/2016 | | 1098 | Purchase QE Invoice | 7,628.00 | 1,525.60 | 9,153.60 | | 9,153.60 |
| 31/03/2016 | | Chq no 100077 | Supplier Payment | | | -1,875.21 | 0.00 | 0.00 |
| | | | | | | 9,153.60 | | 9,153.60 |

**Stationery World (SP04)**

| Date | Number | Reference | Type | Net | VAT | Total | Discount | Outstanding |
|---|---|---|---|---|---|---|---|---|
| 29/02/2016 | | Inv 0187 | Supplier OB Invoice | 9,504.32 | 0.00 | 9,504.32 | | 0.00 |
| 14/03/2016 | | 0197 | Purchase QE Invoice | 3,567.00 | 713.40 | 4,280.40 | | 4,280.40 |
| 19/03/2016 | | RF287 | Purchase QE Credit | -124.08 | -24.82 | -148.90 | | -148.90 |
| 31/03/2016 | | Chq no 100078 | Supplier Payment | | | -9,504.32 | 0.00 | 0.00 |
| | | | | | | 4,131.50 | | 4,131.50 |

## TASK 15

### Trial Balance

From: 29/02/2016
To: 31/03/2016

**Way To Work**
**Trial Balance Report**

12 May 2017
11:13

This period only

| Nominal Code | Name | Selected Period | |
|---|---|---|---|
| | | Debit | Credit |
| 0040 | Fixtures and fittings - Cost | 8,000.00 | |
| 0050 | Motor Vehicles - Cost | 14,000.00 | |
| 1100 | Trade Debtors | 18,474.00 | |
| 1200 | Current | | 2,589.76 |
| 1210 | Petty Cash | 206.68 | |
| 1220 | Deposit | 1,500.00 | |
| 2100 | Trade Creditors | | 20,996.90 |
| 2200 | VAT on Sales | | 2,519.33 |
| 2201 | VAT on Purchases | 2,463.20 | |
| 3200 | Capital introduced | | 34,000.00 |
| 3260 | Drawings - equity | 1,000.00 | |
| 4000 | Stationery Sales | | 7,893.73 |
| 4001 | CD Rom Sales | | 1,776.00 |
| 4002 | Printer Accessories Sales | | 14,527.63 |
| 5000 | Stationery Purchases | 6,331.92 | |
| 5001 | CD Rom Purchases | 555.00 | |
| 5002 | Printer Accessory Purchases | 22,628.00 | |
| 6201 | Advertising | 327.00 | |
| 7000 | Wages and Salaries | 5,600.00 | |
| 7100 | Rent and rates | 2,668.00 | |
| 7200 | Gas and electric | 84.10 | |
| 7900 | Bank charges and interest | 123.45 | |
| 8200 | General Expenses | 342.00 | |
| | TOTAL | €84,303.35 | €84,303.35 |

## TASK 15

## Audit Trail for March (inc opening balances)

From: 29/02/2016
To: 31/03/2016

Way To Work
**Audit Trail Breakdown**

12 May 2017
11:16

Type: All, Status: All

| Trx No | Entry Date | User | Trx Date | Name | Type | Invoice Number | Ref | Ledger Account | Debit | Credit | Bank Reconciled |
|---|---|---|---|---|---|---|---|---|---|---|---|
| 1 | 11/05/2017 | LH | 29/02/2016 | Morgan, Smith & Winston (JP01) | Customer OB Invoice | | INV021 | Opening Balances Control Account (9998) | | 1,172.34 | No |
| | | | | | | | | Trade Debtors (1100) | 1,172.34 | | No |
| 2 | 11/05/2017 | LH | 29/02/2016 | Cyril West (JP02) | Customer OB Invoice | | INV045 | Opening Balances Control Account (9998) | | 2,954.00 | No |
| | | | | | | | | Trade Debtors (1100) | 2,954.00 | | No |
| 3 | 11/05/2017 | LH | 29/02/2016 | Wallace & Gromit Ltd (JP03) | Customer OB Invoice | | INV033 | Opening Balances Control Account (9998) | | 3,180.00 | No |
| | | | | | | | | Trade Debtors (1100) | 3,180.00 | | No |
| 4 | 11/05/2017 | LH | 29/02/2016 | Star Paper (JP04) | Customer OB Invoice | | INV034 | Opening Balances Control Account (9998) | | 1,867.34 | No |
| | | | | | | | | Trade Debtors (1100) | 1,867.34 | | No |
| 5 | 11/05/2017 | LH | 29/02/2016 | Paper Products UK (SP01) | Supplier OB Invoice | | Inv 0165 | Trade Creditors (2100) | | 445.23 | No |
| | | | | | | | | Opening Balances Control Account (9998) | 445.23 | | No |
| 6 | 11/05/2017 | LH | 29/02/2016 | Wallace & Gromit Ltd (SP02) | Supplier OB Invoice | | Inv 02183 | Trade Creditors (2100) | | 6,711.00 | No |
| | | | | | | | | Opening Balances Control Account (9998) | 6,711.00 | | No |
| 7 | 11/05/2017 | LH | 29/02/2016 | Whole Office Furniture (SP03) | Supplier OB Invoice | | Inv 1028 | Trade Creditors (2100) | | 1,875.21 | No |
| | | | | | | | | Opening Balances Control Account (9998) | 1,875.21 | | No |
| 8 | 11/05/2017 | LH | 29/02/2016 | Stationery World (SP04) | Supplier OB Invoice | | Inv 0187 | Trade Creditors (2100) | | 9,504.32 | No |
| | | | | | | | | Opening Balances Control Account (9998) | 9,504.32 | | No |
| 9 | 11/05/2017 | LH | 29/02/2016 | | Bank Opening Balance | | | Opening Balances Control Account (9998) | | 6,210.81 | No |
| | | | | | | | | Current (1200) | 6,210.81 | | Yes |
| 10 | 11/05/2017 | LH | 29/02/2016 | | Bank Opening Balance | | | Opening Balances Control Account (9998) | | 100.00 | No |
| | | | | | | | | Petty Cash (1210) | 100.00 | | No |
| 11 | 11/05/2017 | LH | 29/02/2016 | | Journal Opening Balance | | OB 1/3/16 | Motor Vehicles - Cost (0050) | 14,000.00 | | No |
| | | | | | | | | Opening Balances Control Account (9998) | | 14,000.00 | No |

From: 29/02/2016
To: 31/03/2016

Way To Work
**Audit Trail Breakdown**

12 May 2017
11:16

| | | | | | | | | Ledger Account | Debit | Credit | Bank Reconciled |
|---|---|---|---|---|---|---|---|---|---|---|---|
| | | | | | | | | Fixtures and fittings - Cost (0040) | 8,000.00 | | No |
| | | | | | | | | Opening Balances Control Account (9998) | | 8,000.00 | No |
| | | | | | | | | Capital introduced (3200) | | 34,000.00 | No |
| | | | | | | | | Opening Balances Control Account (9998) | 34,000.00 | | No |
| | | | | | | | | Drawings - equity (3260) | 1,000.00 | | No |
| | | | | | | | | Opening Balances Control Account (9998) | | 1,000.00 | No |
| | | | | | | | | Stationery Sales (4000) | | 903.73 | No |
| | | | | | | | | Opening Balances Control Account (9998) | 903.73 | | No |
| | | | | | | | | CD Rom Sales (4001) | | 855.00 | No |
| | | | | | | | | Opening Balances Control Account (9998) | 855.00 | | No |
| | | | | | | | | Printer Accessories Sales (4002) | | 9,842.00 | No |
| | | | | | | | | Opening Balances Control Account (9998) | 9,842.00 | | No |
| | | | | | | | | Stationery Purchases (5000) | 2,400.00 | | No |
| | | | | | | | | Opening Balances Control Account (9998) | | 2,400.00 | No |
| | | | | | | | | CD Rom Purchases (5001) | 210.00 | | No |
| | | | | | | | | Opening Balances Control Account (9998) | | 210.00 | No |
| | | | | | | | | Printer Accessory Purchases (5002) | 15,000.00 | | No |
| | | | | | | | | Opening Balances Control Account (9998) | | 15,000.00 | No |
| | | | | | | | | Wages and Salaries (7000) | 5,600.00 | | No |
| | | | | | | | | Opening Balances Control Account (9998) | | 5,600.00 | No |
| | | | | | | | | General Expenses (8200) | 342.00 | | No |
| | | | | | | | | Opening Balances Control Account (9998) | | 342.00 | No |
| | | | | | | | | Rent and rates (7100) | 2,100.00 | | No |
| | | | | | | | | Opening Balances Control Account (9998) | | 2,100.00 | No |
| 12 | 11/05/2017 | LH | 01/03/2016 | | Bank Transfer | | TRANS01 | Current (1200) | | 1,500.00 | Yes |
| | | | | | | | | Deposit (1220) | 1,500.00 | | No |

| From: 29/02/2016 To: 31/03/2016 | | | | | Way To Work Audit Trail Breakdown | | | | | | 12 May 2017 11:16 |
|---|---|---|---|---|---|---|---|---|---|---|---|
| 13 | 11/05/2017 | LH | 03/03/2016 | Cyril West (JP02) | Sales QE Invoice | INV041 | Stationery Sales (4000) | | 780.00 | No |
| | | | | | | | VAT on Sales (2200) | | 156.00 | No |
| | | | | | | | Trade Debtors (1100) | 936.00 | | No |
| 14 | 11/05/2017 | LH | 03/03/2016 | Star Paper (JP04) | Sales QE Invoice | INV042 | CD Rom Sales (4001) | | 921.00 | No |
| | | | | | | | VAT on Sales (2200) | | 184.20 | No |
| | | | | | | | Trade Debtors (1100) | 1,105.20 | | No |
| 15 | 11/05/2017 | LH | 05/03/2016 | Morgan, Smith & Winston (JP01) | Sales QE Invoice | INV043 | Printer Accessories Sales (4002) | | 4,376.00 | No |
| | | | | | | | VAT on Sales (2200) | | 875.20 | No |
| | | | | | | | Trade Debtors (1100) | 5,251.20 | | No |
| 16 | 11/05/2017 | LH | 07/03/2016 | Wallace & Gromit Ltd (JP03) | Sales QE Invoice | INV044 | Printer Accessories Sales (4002) | | 458.00 | No |
| | | | | | | | VAT on Sales (2200) | | 91.60 | No |
| | | | | | | | Trade Debtors (1100) | 549.60 | | No |
| 17 | 11/05/2017 | LH | 07/03/2016 | Morgan, Smith & Winston (JP01) | Sales QE Invoice | INV45 | Stationery Sales (4000) | | 6,210.00 | No |
| | | | | | | | VAT on Sales (2200) | | 1,242.00 | No |
| | | | | | | | Trade Debtors (1100) | 7,452.00 | | No |
| 18 | 11/05/2017 | LH | 17/03/2016 | Star Paper (JP04) | Sales QE Credit | CR51 | Trade Debtors (1100) | | 301.52 | No |
| | | | | | | | Printer Accessories Sales (4002) | 251.27 | | No |
| | | | | | | | VAT on Sales (2200) | 50.25 | | No |
| 19 | 11/05/2017 | LH | 10/03/2016 | Paper Products UK (SP01) | Purchase QE Invoice | 0200 | Trade Creditors (2100) | | 586.80 | No |
| | | | | | | | Stationery Purchases (5000) | 489.00 | | No |
| | | | | | | | VAT on Purchases (2201) | 97.80 | | No |
| 20 | 11/05/2017 | LH | 11/03/2016 | Wallace & Gromit Ltd (SP02) | Purchase QE Invoice | 02241 | Trade Creditors (2100) | | 414.00 | No |
| | | | | | | | CD Rom Purchases (5001) | 345.00 | | No |
| | | | | | | | VAT on Purchases (2201) | 69.00 | | No |
| 21 | 11/05/2017 | LH | 11/03/2016 | Whole Office Furniture (SP03) | Purchase QE Invoice | 1098 | Trade Creditors (2100) | | 9,153.60 | No |
| | | | | | | | Printer Accessory Purchases (5002) | 7,628.00 | | No |

Who: Leanne Halsall    Produced by Sage One    Page 3 of 5

| From: 29/02/2016 To: 31/03/2016 | | | | | Way To Work Audit Trail Breakdown | | | | | | 12 May 2017 11:16 |
|---|---|---|---|---|---|---|---|---|---|---|---|
| | | | | | | | VAT on Purchases (2201) | 1,525.60 | | No |
| 22 | 11/05/2017 | LH | 14/03/2016 | Stationery World (SP04) | Purchase QE Invoice | 0197 | Trade Creditors (2100) | | 4,280.40 | No |
| | | | | | | | Stationery Purchases (5000) | 3,567.00 | | No |
| | | | | | | | VAT on Purchases (2201) | 713.40 | | No |
| 23 | 11/05/2017 | LH | 19/03/2016 | Stationery World (SP04) | Purchase QE Credit | RF287 | Stationery Purchases (5000) | | 124.08 | No |
| | | | | | | | VAT on Purchases (2201) | | 24.82 | No |
| | | | | | | | Trade Creditors (2100) | 148.90 | | No |
| 24 | 11/05/2017 | LH | 15/03/2016 | Morgan, Smith & Winston (JP01) | Customer Receipt | Chqno 203998 | Trade Debtors (1100) | | 1,172.34 | No |
| | | | | | | | Current (1200) | 1,172.34 | | Yes |
| 25 | 11/05/2017 | LH | 17/03/2016 | Cyril West (JP02) | Customer Receipt | Chq no 103112 | Trade Debtors (1100) | | 2,954.00 | No |
| | | | | | | | Current (1200) | 2,954.00 | | Yes |
| 26 | 11/05/2017 | LH | 19/03/2016 | Star Paper (JP04) | Customer Receipt | Chq no 011211 | Trade Debtors (1100) | | 1,867.34 | No |
| | | | | | | | Trade Debtors (1100) | 301.52 | | No |
| | | | | | | | Current (1200) | 1,565.82 | | Yes |
| 27 | 11/05/2017 | LH | 31/03/2016 | Paper Products UK (SP01) | Supplier Payment | Chq no 100076 | Trade Creditors (2100) | 445.23 | | No |
| | | | | | | | Current (1200) | | 445.23 | Yes |
| 28 | 11/05/2017 | LH | 31/03/2016 | Whole Office Furniture (SP03) | Supplier Payment | Chq no 100077 | Trade Creditors (2100) | 1,875.21 | | No |
| | | | | | | | Current (1200) | | 1,875.21 | Yes |
| 29 | 11/05/2017 | LH | 31/03/2016 | Stationery World (SP04) | Supplier Payment | Chq no 100078 | Trade Creditors (2100) | 9,504.32 | | No |
| | | | | | | | Current (1200) | | 9,504.32 | No |
| 30 | 11/05/2017 | LH | 15/03/2016 | | Bank Transfer | TRANS02 | Current (1200) | | 600.00 | Yes |
| | | | | | | | Petty Cash (1210) | 600.00 | | No |
| 31 | 11/05/2017 | LH | 19/03/2016 | | Other Payment | Petty cash voucher 056 | Petty Cash (1210) | | 100.92 | No |
| | | | | | | | Gas and electric (7200) | 96.11 | | No |
| | | | | | | | VAT on Purchases (2201) | 4.81 | | No |
| | | | | | | | Petty Cash (1210) | 100.92 | | No |

Who: Leanne Halsall    Produced by Sage One    Page 4 of 5

| From: 29/02/2016 | | | | Way To Work | | | | | | 12 May 2017 | |
| To: 31/03/2016 | | | | Audit Trail Breakdown | | | | | | 11:16 | |

| | | | | | | | | | | | |
|---|---|---|---|---|---|---|---|---|---|---|---|
| | | | | | | | Gas and electric (7200) | | | 96.11 | No |
| | | | | | | | VAT on Purchases (2201) | | | 4.81 | No |
| 32 | 11/05/2017 | LH | 19/03/2016 | | Other Payment | Petty cash voucher 056 | Petty Cash (1210) | | | 100.92 | No |
| | | | | | | | Gas and electric (7200) | 84.10 | | | No |
| | | | | | | | VAT on Purchases (2201) | 16.82 | | | No |
| 33 | 11/05/2017 | LH | 20/03/2016 | | Other Payment | Petty cash voucher 057 | Petty Cash (1210) | | | 392.40 | No |
| | | | | | | | Advertising (6201) | 327.00 | | | No |
| | | | | | | | VAT on Purchases (2201) | 65.40 | | | No |
| 34 | 11/05/2017 | LH | 28/03/2016 | | Other Receipt | ST4 | Printer Accessories Sales (4002) | | | 102.90 | No |
| | | | | | | | VAT on Sales (2200) | | | 20.58 | No |
| | | | | | | | Current (1200) | | 123.48 | | Yes |
| 36 | 11/05/2017 | LH | 31/03/2016 | | Other Payment | standing order rent | Current (1200) | | | 568.00 | Yes |
| | | | | | | | Rent and rates (7100) | 568.00 | | | No |
| | | | | | | | VAT on Purchases (2201) | | | | No |
| 48 | 11/05/2017 | LH | 31/03/2016 | | Bank Payment | Bank Charge | Current (1200) | | | 123.45 | Yes |
| | | | | | | | Bank charges and interest (7900) | 123.45 | | | No |

## TASK 15

## Nominal Ledger Activity for Bank/Petty Cash

| From: 29/02/2016 | | | | Way To Work | | | | | | 12 May 2017 | |
| To: 31/03/2016 | | | | Detailed Nominal Activity | ent (1200) | | | | | 11:07 | |

Transaction Type: All

| Trx No | Date | Invoice Number | Name | Type | Reference | Description | Debit | Credit | Running Total |
|---|---|---|---|---|---|---|---|---|---|
| | | | | | | Opening Balance | | 0.00 | |
| 9 | 29/02/2016 | | | Bank Opening Balance | | | 6,210.81 | | 6,210.81 Dr |
| 12 | 01/03/2016 | | | Bank Transfer | TRANS01 | | | 1,500.00 | 4,710.81 Dr |
| 24 | 15/03/2016 | | Morgan, Smith & Winston (JP01) | Customer Receipt | Chqno 203996 | | 1,172.34 | | 5,883.15 Dr |
| 30 | 15/03/2016 | | | Bank Transfer | TRANS02 | | | 600.00 | 5,283.15 Dr |
| 25 | 17/03/2016 | | Cyril West (JP02) | Customer Receipt | Chq no 103112 | | 2,954.00 | | 8,237.15 Dr |
| 26 | 19/03/2016 | | Star Paper (JP04) | Customer Receipt | Chq no 011211 | | 1,565.82 | | 9,802.97 Dr |
| 34 | 28/03/2016 | | | Other Receipt | ST4 | | 123.48 | | 9,926.45 Dr |
| 27 | 31/03/2016 | | Paper Products UK (SP01) | Supplier Payment | Chq no 100076 | | | 445.23 | 9,481.22 Dr |
| 28 | 31/03/2016 | | Whole Office Furniture (SP03) | Supplier Payment | Chq no 100077 | | | 1,875.21 | 7,606.01 Dr |
| 29 | 31/03/2016 | | Stationery World (SP04) | Supplier Payment | Chq no 100078 | | | 9,504.32 | 1,898.31 Cr |
| 36 | 31/03/2016 | | | Other Payment | standing order rent | | | 568.00 | 2,466.31 Cr |
| 48 | 31/03/2016 | | | Bank Payment | Bank Charge | | | 123.45 | 2,589.76 Cr |
| | | | | | | Closing Balance | | 2,589.76 | |
| | | | | | | Period Variance | | 2,589.76 | |

| From: 29/02/2016 | | | | Way To Work | | | | | | 12 May 2017 | |
| To: 31/03/2016 | | | | Detailed Nominal Activity: Petty Cash (1210) | | | | | | 11:24 | |

Transaction Type: All

| Trx No | Date | Invoice Number | Name | Type | Reference | Description | Debit | Credit | Running Total |
|---|---|---|---|---|---|---|---|---|---|
| | | | | | | Opening Balance | | 0.00 | |
| 10 | 29/02/2016 | | | Bank Opening Balance | | | 100.00 | | 100.00 Dr |
| 30 | 15/03/2016 | | | Bank Transfer | TRANS02 | | 600.00 | | 700.00 Dr |
| 32 | 19/03/2016 | | | Other Payment | Petty cash voucher 056 | | | 100.92 | 599.08 Dr |
| 33 | 20/03/2016 | | | Other Payment | Petty cash voucher 057 | | | 392.40 | 206.68 Dr |
| | | | | | | Closing Balance | 206.68 | | |
| | | | | | | Period Variance | 206.68 | | |

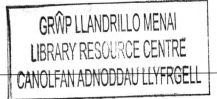